SOMEWHERE DEEP DOWN WHEN

Poetry by Darrell "SCIPOET" Stover

MELOLIPS Cary, NC

ISBN 978-0-557-85912-2

To Creation

For Larry, Amiri, Bob, Sterling and Langston
Jayne, Sonia, Nikki, Zora and Gwendolyn

Thank you to my wife Mary, my daughter Imani,
my son Darius, and the extended family

Special thanks to the libraries, schools,
institutions and individuals who have
believed in me and hosted my work

Big hugs to T.J. Reddy for his art
that graces the cover and
Gail Williams for working it

My writing and performance colleagues over
time and Preston Sampson
for the sketch

Contents

Introduction: The Two DCs

Somewhere deep down when our heroes wore fro's there was Abbey Lincoln, Nina Simone, and Angela Davis don't you know. Somewhere deep down when our heroes wore fro's there was Amiri Baraka, Huey Newton, and Michael Jackson don't you know. Betty Davis, Dr. J, ?uestlove, Erykah Badu, Esperanza Spalding…

This is a celebratory collection of poems scripted and performed in Washington, DC and Durham City of Medicine. They reflect an energized voice saturated in Africanisms, folklore and folk future, percussive and discursive. This volume is long overdue since my first single volume, *Record of the Green Hat Chronicles Volume I* (Metro Lover Lives Press), was published over 20 years ago. Some of these poems have that same age on them. Others are current to just yesterday and some will capture attention in tomorrows to come.

The nation's capitol and its suburbs have a tradition of poetry readings and events etched in my sage memory. Sterling Brown, blues poet and literary scholar, holding court in libraries and on campuses in the 70's and 80's. Gwendolyn Brooks and Rita Dove, both recipients of Pulitzers for their poetry, serving as Poetry Consultant to the Library of Congress and Poet Laureate, respectively in the 80's and 90's. Amiri Baraka paying tribute to Larry Neal and Bob Marley who both passed in 1981 in his poem "Wailers" in 1983 at the Senate Office Building for the Larry Neal Writers Conference. Larry Neal's *HooDoo Hollerin' Bebop Ghosts* (Howard University Press) has been one of my continuous and major inspirations. I am performing "Orishas" from that volume backed by my performance colleagues poet and musician Sydney March on flute and storyteller Morton Brooks on ashiko drum in a tribute to Bob Marley captured in the back cover photo taken by Foodhead aka Harold Finley. Performing and writing in a jazz aesthetic and the griotic tradition remains my perpetual "cool pose" and poetic commitment.

Many innovative literary events took place with my direct development and participation in DC, for example the first Poet on Every Corner (POEC) was held at the intersection of 14th and U streets NW in 1987 under the auspices of the African American Writers Guild. Sharing outdoors with me that day was poetic Coltrane biographer and trauma surgeon C.O. Simpkins, performance poets Kweli Smith and Garth Tate, and Foodhead. That day was immortalized in a color photo essay published in the *Washington Post*. The operative aspect of such events was to have collectives of poets reading outside in dialogue with the general public and in open advertisement of the art from the page to the community with larger statements and significations being made. Successive POECs were held to celebrate Martin Luther King Jr. around the MLK Library (1988), Nelson Mandela from the White House to the South African Embassy (1988), Women of the African Diaspora around the Corcoran Gallery (1989), Juli Dash's "Daughters of the Dust" film showing in Georgetown at Wisconsin Avenue and M Street (1994), and the Harlem Renaissance, the Shaw community and early writers in DC, Sterling Brown, Georgia Douglass Johnson, Paul Lawrence Dunbar, Jean Toomer, Langston Hughes, and May Miller from the Howard Theatre to the Lincoln Theatre as part of the Remembering U Street Festival (1995).

The founding of the Spoken Word Performance Poetry Ensemble in 1988 led to several reading series at Kobos, an African fashion emporium starting in 1990. This ensemble's membership consisted of Joy Jones, Caprece Jackson, Leslie Lewis, Lasana Mack, Kenneth Carroll, and myself. It led to my editing and the publishing of the group's anthology, *Bad Beats Sacred Rhythms* (The Spoken Word) in 1993. The Spoken Word, as the group came to be known in performance, was accompanied by dancer Za'yn McClean and musicians Doc Powell (who orchestrated the drum and poetry connection with the Malcolm X Park Drummers), Butch Jackson, Morton Brooks, reed men Sydney March and Freddie Green, and a busload of others over time.

The Spoken Word Performance Poetry Ensemble, as a collective, presented workshops in schools and on an ongoing basis to this very day at the John Howard Pavillion of the St. Elizabeth's forensic ward. I also maintained an excursion into creative expression primarily for young men in juvenile detention called "Rappin' and Writin" from 1991-1993 through the Fusion Program of the University of the District of Columbia and 1994-1996 through WritersCorp. This workshop instilled in its participants an understanding of rap as poetry connected to an African diasporic oral tradition weaving in history, literature, and the interpretation of rap lyrics. It also encouraged transformation through intellectual growth, self respect, and a rootedness in cultural heritage.

The six day a week juvenile detention center workshops in DC and Laurel, MD took place while I maintained a family in Alexandria, VA, worked as a microbiology and biotechnology senior editor at Cambridge Scientific Abstracts in Bethesda, MD, worked hard on my M.A. in writing at Johns Hopkins University between Baltimore and DC, and directed the Spoken Word. I heeded the words of musician and co-worker Rene' Ibanez, my Cuban hermano. He said, "Yo bro, you need some gigs cause those diapers gonna cost!" This elicited shortly after my daughter, Imani, was born in 1992.

I am reminded of the gigs I got while sitting in Durham's hottest jazz spot, the Be Yu' Bistro and Café, listening to the hottest of trios, James "Saxsmo" Gates on you guessed it, hot handed Brevan Hampden on drums, and quick time fingered Ernest Turner on organ. Back in 1994 I was on mic in the kitchen, Butch Jackson on percussion in the living room, and Taz on sax wired just inside the entry door to this efficiency apartment. What we recorded in Adams Morgan in NW DC led to the vinyl release of "Acousticsoulfulbebopbooms" by Peace Bureau on Eightball Records. Produced by Eric Hilton now of Thievery Corporation and owner of several clubs, including my favorite on 14th Street, Marvin's. The recording was an amalgam of rap, spoken word, jazz, and djing mixed masterfully. What appeared as "Cultural Verses" on the album is included here under its original title, "Culture vs. Computers."

Then came my family's move to North Carolina. As is the case for so many on our planet, we migrate to improve our situation. Our move was to support my wife, Mary, in her then new position in the Triangle. One night in DC before my departure it was suggested to me by Abasi Johnson, formerly of the reggae group Black Sheep who was originally from Jacksonville, NC, that I would see a change in my poetry. New experiences, people, and events to sing the praises of proved him true and me feeling continuously creative and blessed.

The transitional poems that were scripted in DC, but found resonance in Durham and points beyond were first and foremost "Sister Dance" which celebrates dance scholar, anthropologist and choreographer Pearl Primus. This poem served as my introduction to Baba Chuck Davis and the African American Dance Ensemble wherein he invited me in as their resident poet in the fall of 1996. This poem was performed at Baba Chuck's traditional Imani celebration on January 1, 1997 with my daughter, Imani accompanying her father through dance interpretation. The second poem to make the trek and capture intellects here in NC is the go-go music metered "Mad Baby" which I wrote to cue young folks into the environmental sciences as it celebrates botanist JoAnn Burkholder of North Carolina State University, run-off driven fish killing algal blooms, and the microscopic and toxic organism she discovered, *Pfisteria piscicida*. Presented at a water hearing in Raleigh, shared in a TV news piece by Anthony Wilson, and published in the Haw River Assembly newsletter its story didn't end there as you will see later. Thirdly, there was my first blues poem which is published elsewhere, "Screamin' Guitars," which became a mainstay poem performed at the Open Mic Jam Sessions run by Brett Chambers initially at the Talk of the Town and now at Papa Mojo's Roadhouse. Other blues poems popular there are "What the Fingers Do" that celebrates several bluesicians and "Stepped It Up and Gone On" for Blind Boy Fuller. "Hayti, Hayti handed down, handed down…"

The Hayti Heritage Center became my home away from home once I became the Program Director there. I was initially contracted to upgrade programming in congruence with a grant narrative for funding the center as a lead-up to its renovation and reopening. During 1998 to 2002 I instituted "Poetry Power," a program that highlighted local and national writers, especially poets. Some of those writers included members of the Carolina African American Writers Collective, among them Evie Shockley, Victor Blue, Lenard Moore and L. Teresa Church, poet and playwright Howard Craft, science fiction writers Sheree' Thomas and Nalo Hopkinson, scholar Daryl Cumber Dance, Kalamu Ya Salaam, Amiri Baraka, filmmaker and performance poet Michele Parkerson, Rabia Rayford, Abena Disroe, Kenneth Carroll, Joy Jones, and numerous others.

An initial task required me to reinstitute and reinvigorate the Tinker Toy Theater, an adult performance ensemble interpreting children's literature to raise the emphasis on reading and love for books in pre-schoolers through early elementary school students. The choreopoem "Which Anancy Are You?" became the introduction to Rhyme Time presentations to audiences in day cares, schools, and libraries as Jackie Marriott, Angela Ray, myself and others, dressed in exquisite spider costumes, excited many through Anancy storytelling extravaganzas with Charles Streeter as narrator. Fast forward. A young woman unmasked me as the Green and Purple Anancy one day at the Bull Durham Blues Festival as she went on to say she took the message seriously enough to stick to reading and writing, now matriculating as a journalism major in college. Makes you wanna cry.

I also refitted the Black Diaspora Film Festival in ways that matched the award-winning blues programming of "Hayti," so in 1999 there was "Celluloid Sounds: Black Music Traditions through Film." This featured a poetic tribute by Brothers with Vision, a center supported performance ensemble, to Sterling Brown, scholar and blues poet, with a panel featuring James Madison University professor Joanne Gabbin and filmmaker Haile Gerima. The film festival of 2000 was entitled "Must Be Deep: Black Identity through Film Beyond the Stereotypes." It provided the inspiration for "How Deep Can You Be?" which was performed often as an opening introduction to each of the almost ten days of film.

Back to "Mad Baby." The Hayti Heritage Center had been chosen to represent North Carolina in a national celebration of the new millennium. Composer Tony Small was selected to engage the community in a summer long youth science camp residency resulting in a celebration of science in the Triangle. He scripted a musical that incorporated "Mad Baby" replete with go-go percussion (thanks to Allen Redd) and James Brown funkiness. But Small's amazing success was topped off with arranging a studio recording of the soundtrack to the musical, "ScienceQuest," at Walter Hill's studio with the children, local musicians, and a choir! This endeavor could not have happened without the kids, songstress Jasme' Kelly as camp director, dance dean Toya Chinfloo's choreography, and Mama Candace Staten's costumes!

I have been on a blues/jazz/funk blessed journey that gave me the opportunity to present "Is the Beat," a poem in tribute to composer and jazz drummer Max Roach to him at the Duke Ellington School for the Arts in DC in 1993. At the Hayti Heritage Center in 2001 I presented to Pharoah Sanders his celebratory poem "Witness At the Center of the Fire Funnel." The jazz poetry committed soul that I am partnered with the Ira Wiggins Quartet, he the director of the vital and superb jazz program at North Carolina Central University, to perform a jazz and poetry tribute to John Coltrane at the NC Museum of History in 2004. That performance included "Coltrane Poem" at the beginning and "Coltrane's Come and Gone On/You Wanna Go Ascending?" as the finale. Oh yeah, don't let me forget to mention when Butch Jackson and I performed with George Clinton and the P-Funk All Stars bringing in the New Year of 1995 in DC with "Too Funky, Tooo Funky" at the Warner Theater!

The most remarkable and rewarding experience I have had in NC through my poetry occurred through working with the men of Phoenix House, one component of Housing for New Hope. This transition home gives the homeless and men looking for a fresh start in life a process by which to succeed. I was asked to do a workshop back in 1999 and over the years returned to engage in the utilization of creative expression to positively impact residents there. On many occasions I would ask the brothers did they want to publicly share their poems written in our workshops. Most times the answer was no, but one group stepped up to the plate big time in 2006. We had looked at our lives as movies and identified the songs that would appear in the soundtrack. I utilized Gil Scott-Heron as our focus on life and poetry. The poem, "I Saw Gil," set the stage for discussion and creativity revealing the inner core of our being with openness and trust. Each of us shared a story connected to a song and artist that captured a significant period in our lives. These stories and songs became the performance "Flightsongs of the Phoenix." Joan Wade brought along her poetry and masterful choreography and Kim Arrington topped it off with her poetry, spirit, and musicality. The performance was so much a success that we boogied down at the end and did an encore performance a few months later with an emphasis on identifying the music and aspects of the life of Marvin Gaye that resonated with each of us. Where ever you guys are – Thank You God Be With You and Be Strong!

Most of these poems and others you will find inside. One more story if I may. "Run on Water: Td's Tale" is an epic poem resulting from my investigations and travels in coastal North Carolina as inspired by David Cecelski's *The Waterman's Song* (UNC Press) and my life-time interest and study of the Civil War. The poem carries you through the black experience during the Civil War in coastal North Carolina. The poem took on a life of its own once I started to film a short cinematic interpretation of it in 2003. It was dramatized as a central component of a 14 part radio series hosted by me interviewing various historians examining the natural and human history during the focal period of the poem on WNCU 90.7FM. The radio show led to the staging of two multimedia performances (2004 and 2005) featuring Thomasi McDonald, Jackie Marriott, Morton Brooks, and my son Darius, because teachers wanted something they could present to their students. For that it required adding C.R. Gibbs lecturing on US Colored Troops in NC and the scripting of two more epic poems, "Run on Water: Jenna's Tale" and "Run on Water: Toby's Tales of Td" (neither included in this collection) to complete the saga of Td's search for his wife and son from the Dismal Swamp in 1859 to Fort Fisher, Raleigh, and Roanoke Island in 1865.

May your search for self be continuously successful and your journey be empowering to others and open to the inspiration of those who have gone before via the African diasporic principles of SANKOFA and KUJICHAGULIA.

I have been known as THE-MAN-IN-THE-GREEN-HAT in DC, VA and MD, since my arrival in NC it has been SCIPOET. This collection allows you to enjoy both.

Darrell Stover

Somewhere on the train between Cary and Greensboro, NC

December 2011

Be Deep

AXE'

Never Die In Bahia

Eshu laughs at the raven on your chest
You probably thought you've danced your last Carnaval
Bright REDS and YELLOWS jiggle/walk the boulevards
Drums bang BLUE splashes to settle in your hips
But Yemenja's sea breeze you are to breathe no more
Unless
Unless of course
You wish to trade lies with the orishas
And see who makes who chuckle
Tell you what
When you last left Rio
There were no people on the beach
Where were they that morning, afternoon
And soft, YELLOW evening?
Had they all arrived at your funeral too soon?
A GREEN and ORANGE frog you never ate
Awaits an answer
Sleep will never greet your eyes in death
Not here
Not when nightlife screams BLACK
And you've seen stranger things here than in your dreams
Who wants to see an endless dream
When they can see this?
An old, legless man dances the steps of a younger man
With a woman whose beauty
Has never appeared on this sphere before
Her beauty was not only in her smile
But in the way she wore a multi-hued skirt
Draping a figure godly in its aura
Sinful in its sensuality
A flash

A man
Athletic fine
Romantic intellect leaves you crying
Has now taken her place
The old man is now an older woman
Strobing life light to you
As your eyes open on an empty beach
Waves wash up the smells and colors of the freshest bouquets
Contemplate death and you die
The Tropic of Celebration is where that frog lives
And it knows life is Carnaval
She wants to know do you.

Mad Baby

for JoAnn Burkholder – Botanist/Battler of the Ambush-Predator

Huffin and puffin'
Pokin' out your tongue
Don't wanna go to bed
Just have some fun
Mad Baby
Mad Baby

Too much of one
Not enough of the other
Yeah, too much sugar
And not enough lovin'
Mad Baby
Mad Baby

Fast, mass material wants
McDonald's feedin' the brain
TV, games, computers
Drivin' kids insane
Mad Baby
Mad Baby

Cheated
Left out
Misunderstood
Sacrificed in a world of no good
Mad Baby
Mad Baby

Got another Mad Baby
New story to tell
Another Mad Baby
From a watery hell

Down in Carolina
Along its river shores
A new thing is breeding
And its coming to yours

Pfiesteria piscicida
Is its name
Ambush-predator
Its claim to fame

Fish swim over
Mad Baby bubbles out
Plenty fish will die
Ain't no doubt

Mad Baby feeds
On dead fish flesh
More Mad Baby seeds
Ever stronger it gets

24 forms
A new Alien beast
Toxic forms
Microscopic like yeast

Neurotoxins
This dinoflagellate
Suffocates fish
And makes you forget

Environment quickly changin'
Tons of sewage and such

Sick rivers gettin' sicker
Makin' Mad Baby muck

Scientists studied
This bottom brew
Mad Baby was waitin'
And it got them too

Punches in and sucks
Insides of cells
Like a mad vampire
Then it swirls and swells

Strangely disappears
After damage is done
Had its dinner
Had its fun

Mad Baby blooms
Come and go
Will they ever stop
We may never know

Plant scientist
To the rescue
She discovered Mad Baby
All credit is due

In microscopes
Research goes on
Piecing together truth
And what must be done

Give the kids a clean planet
Show them both some love
How would you rather have it?
Ain't you had enough?

Mad Baby
Mad Baby
Let me see you do the Mad Baby y'all
Let me see you do the Mad Baby y'all
Let me see you do the Mad Baby y'all
Mad Baby

Remembering U Street Festival & The Spoken Word

Presents

A POET ON EVERY CORNER

From

HOWARD THEATRE TO LINCOLN THEATRE

An Open Poetry Reading Outside

Saturday, September 30, 1995
at 1:30 PM
7th and T Streets, NW
Washington DC

Celebrating: Sterling Brown, Langston Hughes, Georgia Douglass Johnson, Paul Lawrence Dunbar, Jean Toomer, and May Miller

Featuring: Brandon Johnson • Danny Boylan II • Donna & Danna Kiel • Corinne Goldsmith• Kahlil Gross • Malik-Ben Abraham • Charles McCain • Patrick Washington • Christina Northern • Stephen Russell • Toni Lightfoot • Jane Abersdeston • Darrell Stover • M'Wile Askari • Peggy "Abena" Disroe • Lasana • Joy Jones • Sydney March • Foodhead • Debra Williams-Garner • Eric Antonio • Judy Cohall • John "Butch" Snipes • Morton Brooks • Butch Jackson • and other poets and musicians

Nap "Don't Forget the Blues" Turner will kick-off the Tour
For Info Call 703-723-2620 or 202-279-5414

Ethnopharmacology of Snake Bite Cures

Hedychium stem paste with garlic
Tacca tuber scrapings
Simaba fruit infusion
Ziziphus leaf juice
Rubus flowers unknown

You paved over some good bush
and oh so many snakebite cures have been lost
like colonial rosehips stolen from native arboreta.
The sting of fang stops the brain
Unless a spirit world tripper
applies the proper plant salve.
A swollen ankle, purple and pulsating,
awaits the spit of jungle brew.
An early earth garden,
An ethnobotanist's dream,
sits in some places unseen,
untouched except by the blessed hands of the shaman.
Extraction soaked leaf applied to thigh
says you will not die, but do not try
to steal the elixir.
Caterpillar tractors bite the land
and swallow tons of unearthed minerals.
Monstrous chains coil around trees as fire burns bark.
The cures we need are for a venomous breed of man.
Picture the deity of life
holding the surgeon knife
and a long brown stem in the other hand.
The plants are silent, dead and disappeared
and the deity throws her hands up in surrender.

The operation is over.
The wealthy man dies.
His money can't buy good health,
only more and more of greed's greatest construction,
the destruction of Gaia's balance and sustenance.
The wellspring of knowledge
deep in the genes of the jungle college
repose in the souls of rain forest people.
Indonesia. The Congo. Amazonia.
Where did they all go?
You do not deserve their magic.
You do not know their pain.
The forests are now broken down towns,
uncivilized cities.
The earth screams an echoing curse
of dead soil, plants and cures.
Plagues of migratory mosquitoes,
resistant malarias,
and vengeful viruses
spew forth.
The blue and green ball fries.
The planet, she dies.
Datura root bark paste with cow urine.
Philodendron leaves with beer.
Piper nigrum seed paste with ghee.
Calathea root decoction.
Goodyera leaf paste.
Cissampelos root juice.
Ocimum twigs unknown.

Rap and Roar

Said the signefyin' monkey
and the cool saint
Oscar Brown Jr.
to the lion one day,
"You can rap and roar,
but can you sing?
'Cause Luther Vandross is dead
and we could use
some more love songs,
some singers of love songs,
some tuned lips,
some passion mouths,
some heart guts,
not no poo butts,
nah definitely
not no poo butts."

Luther is gone on
and we gots to have
some potent love crooners
like you and fifty
hundred other
penny-ante manchilds
who only know rap,
but got the blood memory
to lay it out strong and true
like dat dere Ossie Davis did to Ruby Dee,
Billy Dee Williams did to Diana Ross,
and Dr. King did to Coretta.
Put that preacher rap on her.
Just that we want it sung

like Donny Hathaway to Roberta
so all of us
can act up in love
like Will Smith and Jada.

Yeah you can rap and roar,
but tell me
can you sing
Nat King Cole
Frankie Lyman
Jackie Wilson
Sam Cooke
Marvin Gaye
Ray like?
'Cause they,
like Luther,
blew down.
Cried out
with no whining
when the struggle was on
and we needed it then
like we need it
right now.
Ain't nothing changed.
Come on sing
you New Jack frog tenors
on the doo-wop corners
of our pistol-plagued
pond streets,
cricket sopranos
fiddlin' with sisters' souls

sittin' in the concert pews
holdin' tight to radios,
ipods and portable CD's
swoonin'
to church smooth whispers.
No noise boys
just soulful sweet spot
deep heat music
coolin' our desires.

You can rap and roar,
but can you sing
some cat daddy love songs?
'Cause Luther Vandross
has passed on
to leave you space
for your gut-bucket
up from the bottom
of where you came from,
a Paul Robeson freedom demanding
deep woooo
uooooo
uoooooo
woooooooo
baritone bass
puttin' boogie in our nod
and grace in our night life
denying strife.
He,
who sported
glow tuxes and wizard ties
dazzle-grooved
rhythm and blues magic
stealthily imparted
on our shifting auras,
a powerful juju jazz

for romance
so instinctively
absorbed by our souls.

Ah yes.
You can rap and roar,
but can you sing
a new soft blues,
something like you heard
when your ears first worked
in the echo chamber
of the womb,
peacefully wet,
quiet,
yet bathed in the orchestra
of your momma's
heart throbs and blood flows?
Sing us something we can feel
down to our pedicure-needin' toes.

Yes, yes.
You can rap and roar,
but can you sing?
'Cause Luther is gone
and what we need,
what we really need
is the bombtastic love,
an all powerful
'keep the faith baby' love.
Can you love/sing,
harmonize outside the key of bling bling
with the notes of yes I can can?
Sing love to the sisters.
Sing love to the brothers.
Sing love to all babies, fathers and mothers.
Sing love to yourselves.

Spit some love.
Spray some love.
Rhyme some love.
Give up some stupid love.
Get your rap on
and be loved
roarin',
"Luther Vandross you up there,
but I got your back down here, baby.
I heard the signefyin' monkey
and the poet-warrior
Oscar Brown Jr.
say to this lion one day,
'There's a fine,
sweet honey queen
down the way.'
Luther's passed
and she wants to hear
this courageous king
sing out about
Love Love, Love Love
Forever, For always, For love."
Yeaaaeaahh!

Jam Band Party Parade

For the Raleigh Helping Hands Mission Marching Band

Doom Boom Ba Doom Boom(3X)

Stars and superstars
swirl in their black
and golden mix
of martial music mayhem.
If they ain't in your parade
you ain't got one.
Naw son.
You ain't got one
like one fish
ain't no school.
No drum trumpets,
floats and goats
gonna get it
goin'on,
unless,
not unless
they there,
right there.

Doom Boom Ba Doom Boom(3X)

Swiggle wiggle.
Dip.
Circle shake.
Snake hip squirm.
Beat.
March step.
Beat.

March on a quarter block.
Do it again.
Beat a quarter block.
High step
and do it again
go-go style.

Doom Boom Ba Doom Boom(3X)

Pretty gals smile
all the while
hump pumpin'
hot jiggle wigglin'
gettin' fancy
in their prance and dance.
Brown indigo honey
step timin' to the beat
ladeedadee hand waves
and gravity-defyin' leans
mean as they wanna be.

Doom Boom Ba Doom Boom(3X)

Bringin' that bottom
up from their backsides
tuba boys and drummers
chat happy with trumpet singers
as drum major step daddies
skyyyyyyyyyyyyyyyyyy
highhhhhhhhhhhhhhh
then drop it to a split!
Crowd howls and follows
your spiritedness,
your raw and eternal
faith in ministerin'
movement and music
movement and music.
I said

ministerin'
movement and music
for holidays
for helpin' souls
be youthful souls
again and again
community steppin' to the beat
go-go style.

Doom Boom Ba Doom Boom(3X)

If they ain't in your parade,
You
ain't
got one,
son!

"FLIGHTSONGS OF THE PHOENIX"

Saturday, February 25, 2006 7:00 PM

Hayti Heritage Center

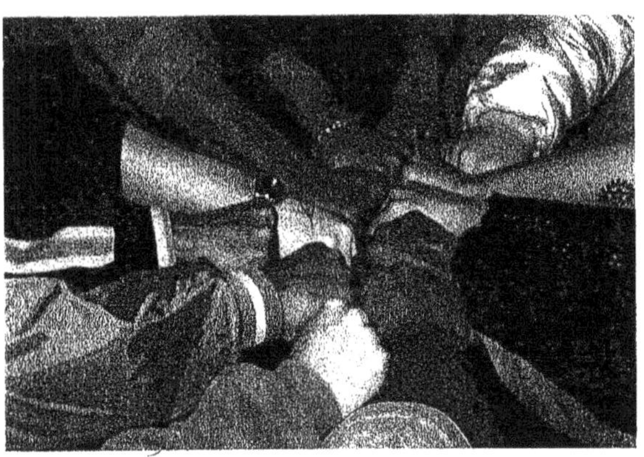

A night of collective storytelling, poetry, song and movement featuring the **Men of Phoenix House** along with **Darrell Stover** (performance poet), **Kim Arrington** (poet and singer) and **Joan Wade** (poet and choreographer)

The Phoenix House is a successful transition home for men in Durham that was started in 1992 by Housing for New Hope. Darrell Stover has been presenting creative expression workshops there since 1999. These workshops contribute to the life transformation and healing that is a hallmark for the men at Phoenix House. Poetry and seeing one's life as a film sets the stage for identifying the music for the soundtrack of their lives. The performance will examine soul, r & b, funk, rap and the socio-political jazz and poetry of Gil Scott- Heron, a part of the transformative process. This event is free and open to the public.

For more information call (919) 683-1709 or www.hayti.org

Dear Precious Daughter of Dunn

For Helen "Xiney" Brown

Wow,
what fun you can be
when you see the wonder in the world.
Wow us Xiney!
A future clear as bright sunrays
is the vision of the Ancients you give us,
majestic in their finery.
You weave wonder.
Fabrics dance to your commandments.
Wow Xiney!
Patrick and Paris.
You go places
continental citizen,
Earth trippin'
Sister of the Gullah terrain
of Carolina North.
You go places girl,
savior and samaritan,
spread mojos of help.
Harrisburg, PA brought you up
with a familial fertile texture
of souls sweet
as mountain air there,
of souls sweet like yours
nurtured in the distance
of tobacco/textile lands.
You go places woman,
spin myth into sho' nuff
spicey experiences

as DC and NC chant loud
your mystical legacy
today and tomorrows to come.
The sweet spirit of you sings
the tender jubilee
of another of NC's daughters,
Nina
gathered in the glow
of your spectral creations.
Nina Simone sang out
star-filled night hymns,
colorful in your adornments.
Bless us too
in finery
cloth doctor,
alchemist revealer
of the precise science
of cotton, wool and silk.
Who are these many sistren
gracing stages
and brethren doing the same
bounce, shimmy and sashay
inspired in your thread doings?
The Ancients live in them
due to you,
the vessel of pageants past reborn!
The Ancients brought back
through Xineyology,
not Jurassic Park,
not Disneyland,
but Antiquity Alive!
Your technological savvy
prestidigitates the past into the present!
No zippers.
No buttons.
No belts.

Magic Momma,
it always wears well
and sings out
gloriously loud
in its sway and glide,
a seafood banquet
of your smooth/cool songs,
tasty,
a seamless jazziness
of art to wear and feel,
your creative world a galactic gallery.
Romare Bearden be proud!
We got it really goin' on
when we strut
draped to the nines by you
and you ain't gone
each time we put it on.
Back in time,
fast forward
to where you left us
that smile,
that love, that you,
beautiful, ever beautiful,
Oh Precious Daughter of Dunn.

Run on Water: Td's Tale

My name is Td.
I'm a two-times-captured,
North Carolina runaway slave
looking for my wife and son.

Got tired
of toiling timber and turpentine
in the great mucky,
a dismal swamp
distractin' my pain.
Seen many a man
takin' down by gators,
washed away
in storms of upturned seas.

Longed for my family
sold
again and again
in 1859.
A whisper in the wind
spoke of many plantations,
their forced migrations.
Left that swamp
to fill the hole in my heart.
Ran off
looking for my wife and son.
Wandered after these whispers
on and on
along the edges of plantations
that never had seen them.
Heard strange whispers of war,

whispers in the hollow
said don't stop,
follow.

Let my guard down
in my heartbroken state.
Got caught,
creepin' too loud.
Taken to New Bern,
where I first heard
whispers of Abraham,
then on to a boat
to Beaufort.
Water, Toby and I
became good friends.
Knots for nets and sailin',
fishin' and shrimpin'
took my mind
off the missin' place
in my soul.
Not long though.
Whispers again of Abraham
rolled on the tongues of many.
No missin' it
the way it came
off the water.
Abraham comin'.
The whispers,
the whispers of Abraham
had a boldness
as if he the second coming

of the Lord Jesus.
Heard this Abraham
had escaped this place
and was coming back
with the war.

Been a year
I been here.
War gettin' ever closer.
A hustle was about.
Boats in and out
quick.
Trains packed
steamed inland.
Still, quiet nights
came and went.
One of them
Toby told me to come on.
Said they was gonna
steal away
just like Abraham.
Board some ship.
Steal away.
Said they'd be back
just like Abraham.
I told him to go on.
Steal away.
I still gotta find
my wife and son.
Toby and them
went northeast
to freedom
that night,
I deeper south
following whispers
of hope.

Cornered,
beat down
by the homeguard.
Young boys
and old crusty militias,
only men left,
deputized
to serve the state
and Confederacy
as slave chasers,
deserter turners,
judge, jury
and executioners.
Impressed me
into a harsher service.
Herded me,
tied and chained
like 200 others,
down country
to stacking shell upon shell,
shoveling sand and soil,
hoisting timbers
on this man's
god forsaken
piece of land
between the ocean
and Cape Fear River.

Fort Fisher
they called it.
Fort Fisher,
the southerners'
pride and protection
for their special
and final seaport,
Wilmington.

Fort Fisher,
a mountain,
mounted with cannons,
monstrous.
Built by me
and many other lost souls.
Damn near two years
of sand and sea,
salt and sun,
bloody spirit
torn from us
to keep blockade runners
streamin' up and down
the Cape Fear.
Any Union navy
dare these shoals
would feel the fire spit
rage of Fort Fisher.

I been up river
on built up trust.
Workin' Wilmington docks,
wanderin' streets.
Never seen
so many happy people.
Money, booze
and anything you choose.
Dancin' man
skips up to me,
arms and pockets
full of pretty gloves,
whiskey and rum,
waving fancy, white
ladies' bloomers
in my face.
"Make a lady proud,"

he says,
as I took it
in my thick hands.
"Make a lady proud."
He shoves my clasped hands
and the garment
up into my chest.
I clutch it
close to my heart,
thinking hard
on that one day
I find my lady.
I quietly ask,
"How much?"
My reply to his
"Whatcha got?"
is turned out pockets,
empty,
except pieces
of fancy candy
got at the dock.
He takes one piece
and presses
that precious cloth
deeper
into my dreams and pining.
Make a lady proud, boy.
Make a lady proud.

Christmas almost upon us,
but no happiness, here,
not at Fort Fisher.
Got word
a bigger navy coming.
We were all sent
across the river.

Christmas eve night
we heard the booms,
saw explosions
flash like lightning.
Felt rumbles
in the smoky air.
Christmas morning,
a gift
I didn't want to give,
shoveling
sand,
shells
and soil
back into place.
Union
destroyed a flagpole
and that was it.
I squeezed hard
on that garment
tucked in my ragged shirt
and cried my own quiet sea.

Not too long after,
1864 into 1865,
January chill
brought back
a colder resolve,
a grander Union fleet.
No quarter
and no foolin',
they blew up men,
cannons,
and that massive
sand castle.
I was there to see,
smell and survive

that horror.
Fort Fisher,
assailed from sea,
then stormed,
surrendered its pride.
Daybreak found me,
shoveling sand
over Confederate dead.
The whispers came,
quietly then louder.
The whispers
called out my name.
The whispers
got so loud
I looked to see...Toby.
It was Toby
in a military jacket,
with a rifle,
and dozens like him.
Colored troops.
Toby.
Bright buttons.
Toby.
He told me it was over.
I could go with him now.
No, it's not over,
I told him
as the last shovel full of sand
fell on that Confederate grave.
It's just beginning.

My name is Td.
I'm a two-times-captured,
North Carolina runaway slave
looking
for my wife and son.

What It Was

I never saw "Mississippi Burning,"
but I smelled it.
Tupelo '77
we were 18 plus
by freight vans not bus,
children of Rosa
conjoined in an up south experiment,
Maryland college rads,
black and white
seeds of integration
on a mission of witness
to a place in need of truth's power.
Sleep carried us there
wrapped in blankets,
zippered bags,
our convictions and dreams
preferred.

Was Mississippi burning again?
"Yes Lord, yes,"
Fannie Lou Hamer screamed out
all through its history
of un-weeded hate,
agro-oppression
and piss poor ignorance.
A reviled hood and cross
blazed hearth
and left homes smoldering,
a troubled past still unfolding.
Most print never said much,
most authorities the same,

same sheet,
same shame.

Don't go?
Consider the consequences
inaction nurtures.
Deep-rooted sprouts of pain
and potent plague-dog racism,
an infectious fever of rights denied
spread a yellow ooze against humanity.
Consider the necessary antibiotic.
Don't go?
Consider it done.
Take guns?
Take guns you offer.
No, brother.
Although I realized
I must have been crazy
as we turned the corner
of our early spring quest
to see seas of white
kids and women
brandishing boards,
spitting filth
backed by hooded gangs
automatically armed.

This was not south Central
or southeast DC.
It was the deep south.
Stopped and searched.
Stopped and searched

twice on our way
in Tennessee
and just into Mississippi,
Elvis's home state,
Tupelo his home town,
u-shaped for convenient segregation,
a Richard Pryor scenario in real time.
Take guns.
Stopped and searched
would end the quest,
the lessons and blessings
exchanged in struggle,
sung along charred streets
as hands clapped and clasped
became a fisted front
fingering the brotherhood
heritage of Klan and cop
perched on rooftops
and front porch police stations
hidden behind their law
no more.
Next time
we take
NC Robert Williams' global legacy,
a gun-backed fortitude,
more of us and whatever it takes.

A READING CELEBRATING

NELSON MANDELA

PLACE: Lamond-Riggs Public Library
5401 South Dakota Ave. N.E.

TIME: 1:00 p.m.

DATE: Saturday, March 10, 1990

FEATURED POETS:

Wanda Windbush
Trevor Cole
Jennifer E. Smith
Brian Gilmore
Darrell Stover

Mandela's welcome home

Coltrane's Come and Gone On/ You Wanna Go Ascending?

COLTRANE IS GOD! COLTRANE IS GOD!
COLTRANE IS GOD! COLTRANE IS GOD!
Our spiritual selves get a kick and rise skyward
Heavens will be visited by us
Blue Black Bronze Brown Bebop Beat Soul Beings
Blue Black Bronze Brown Bebop Beat Soul Beings
Cherishing vibes screamed out from long ago to echo
When we need them most
We will spiral on
Sound electrons
Charged to move on in our own way
Defined in the notes' groove
This music coalesces into the totality of everybody's love
Something so, so deep and heavy that this Universe is only
A drop in its maelstrom
Monstrous convulsions
Initiated in the howls of a horn
It's too, too late to muffle
The reverb alone has shattered stars
Ever increasing pieces of light
Beyond our own galaxy
We see them through telescopes
Wonder how
How in the extreme chaos of things
Did the stars hear the call
Dissipate into the eternal flow
Coltrane's piping shock waves
Yeah John hit that rest stop for the feeble-hearted
Let them gather their pieces in black hole valleys
Slow the pace with a ballad

From back there in the before time
Bring it up
Bring it on up from your belly and
BREAEAEAEAEAEAEAEAEAEEEEETHE MAN
CIRCULATE AIR
BLOWOWOWOWOWOWOWOWOWOWOWOWOOWW
BROTHER
YEAH BABY, BLOW US ON YOUR HOLY WAY!
COLTRANE IS GOD! COLTRANE IS GOD!
COLTRANE IS GOD! COLTRANE IS GOD!
GOD! GOD! GOD! GOD! GOD! GOD!
Down the hollow tube of a microscope
Mirrored light reflecting the essence of all things made
Gave us the cellular
Gave us the molecular
Gave us the science of saxing
Look down the tube
Every element a Coltrane
The minutest point
The tiniest piece of anything and everything
You look in the eyepiece and there they stand
Saxes in hand - Coltranes
Millions upon millions of the ultimate jazz man
Put them together
Sound abounds
Louder, Wailin', Shimmerin' the atmosphere
Sun dance, moon boogaloo and stars twinkle wildly
As our souls flash, flip-flop, jump, skank, sliiiiiide
Through millennia beyond time's end
Riding the ozone to a higher home

Listen and Go, Listen and Go, Listen and Go!
COLTRANE IS GOD! COLTRANE IS GOD!
COLTRANE IS GOD!
GOD! GOD! GOD! GOD! GOD! GOD!
GO ON! GO ON!
HEAR IT IN YOUR HEART AND GO ON!
COLTRANE IS GOD! COLTRANE IS GOD!
COLTRANE IS GOD!
GOD! GOD!
GOD! GOD!
GOD!

I Saw Gil

Urban bush battle bred ancient songster
Breezin' through the rebel 'me'
Carried sounds of the resistance
Voice piano Nommo
Traditional notifyin' and signefyin'
Through your words we laughed at the water antics
Wetting the gates of White Houses and Capitol domes
The lies flowing like so much prohibition booze
Presidents peeing on themselves in shame
You called their names
Their macho myths dissolved
Your rhythms fought and won wars
Many artists were never drafted for
Groping and squirming
Pimped on the contract deal corner
You never turned your back
When our minds cried out
Like hands reaching out
From a homeless son or daughter
Seeking salvation from this chilly bottle full of Babylon
Shaman whipped up a healing beat
Chanted no retreat no defeat
Only reliance on inner strength
Fortified in your voice ringing out
Rally cries brought forth and through
Fellow challengers to the misbegotten throne
Its legs tilted and tottered
Unleashed truth untelevised
Round midnight banners unfurled in swirled cadence
A hoodooer at the walls of Jericho
Percusses prophet babble

Poured verbs upon verbs
Adjectives, adverbs, and images
Giving sight to our blind tolerance of injustice
Blinking, winking, and nodding to the beat
We See Now
We Chant Loud
"What's the Word?"
"Johannesburg!"
"What's that Music?"
"Storm Music!"
Taking blasts from Ray Guns
We stand firm
Radiate a ritual romance with resistance dance
Put distance between the conscious us
And ignorant things
We saw Gil
We heard Gil
We becomes I
The total combinations of our pleasure and pride
An all-knowingness takes over inside
Mardi gras-ed musical meanness
Metamorphosis of complacency
To civildisobebadidiocy
Cool to hot
Blue to red
Dancin' blood pumps
Shimmerin' hips of revolution
Fire winged humans fly on blues bomb raids
Powered by DO tunes
Sendin' WAKE UP tones
SCREAMS YELLS STOMPS ZIPS ZOOMS

S
T
O
P
!

Hurt hearts ache in the absence of your soul
Where did it all go?
The prophet has passed on
Crucified now by success
His psalms to us are on record
Our psalms to him are yet to be sung
The bullet in the back of Henry Dumas
Has not visited him
The fire in his heart unlike Larry Neal
Has not been dowsed
What keeps the fire burning
Is a strange mix of earth and air
Earth, she is sick
The air polluted
The doctors are on vacation
I saw Gil coming down the hill
Bag in hand
Was it full of hot, steamed crabs
Crack, smack or cures?
I saw Gil in his poetry
And Gil, the man, just yesterday
Asked myself
What happens when the poet's pen runs dry?
Was the life that you always stayed ahead of
Now the loser in the long distance run?
Lungs choked by a tired spirit
Mind torn by visions of too much hypocrisy
Settlin' into a nonchalant daze
I saw Gil and wondered the epitaph
As I let loose a disturbed laugh
A wild stallion studded continues to produce
Even holds one or two more good runs
Doesn't it?
A good father passes on to his daughters and sons
What he has won
Doesn't he?

I saw Gil crack a smile
Before his voice boomed baritone
The questions still went unanswered
Tonal memories reverb
The power of past performance
'The Now' of our struggle calls the tune!

A Tribute to John Coltrane

Jazz and Poetry Concert

Darrell Stover

The Ira Wiggins Quartet
Paul Ingbretsen
Russell Lacy
Ed Paolatonio
Ira Wiggins

September 12, 2004
3 p.m.

Cosponsored by WNCU 90.7 FM.
Program funding provided by GlaxoSmithKline.

5 East Edenton St., Raleigh
919-807-7900
www.ncmuseumofhistory.org

Office of Archives and History
Department of Cultural Resources

NORTH CAROLINA
MUSEUM OF HISTORY

www.wncu.org

Too Too Late

He poured it in the sewer
As the police arrived
Like so many pigeons to crumbs
Where is it
They yelled in bellicose tones of bravado
Guns drawn
Eyes wide
The chase had been breathtaking
Over rooftops and through alleyways
Decorated with America's most unwanted
Massive by-product
Waste
The newspapers mixed with the garbage of last night
At least what the dogs, cats, roaches, and rats
Hadn't devoured
Disrupted by the passing feet,
Cars and helicopter search lights
People looked out windows unto surroundings
They had grown to expect
No more shots rang out this night
The guns had been emptied
Trigger mechanisms overworked
All drugs sold and dispensed
Mental excursions completed
With cries for a more prolonged escape
Everything grew real still
The sun appeared
Rose in the west
Set in the east for forty days and nights
Then the planet was no more
There was not enough time to realize

That it had fallen out of galaxial orbit
They had no true means of escape
Very far away in another time
An alien chemist passes judgement
On a wildly crafted vase
Containing an even stranger liquid
Totalitarian authorities break into his lab
Order him to hand over the vase and its contents
He drinks it
The planet's double suns explode
Engulf everything in their orbit
As the chemist dies at the end of a horrible interrogation
His last words
As their atmosphere vaporizes to whiteness
Reveal the elixir to be a volatile explosive
Endlessly leapfrogging universes
Through the magic of temporal shift
A smudgy label on the bottom of the vase reads
Dispose in the core of the nearest red dwarf star
Or experience the annihilation of your galaxy
Patent pending - Haliburton Acme Weapons System Division
Filing Date June 18, 2006

Ethnomathematics of Braids

For Gloria Gilmer, mathematician and Howard L. Craft,
Playwright/calculator of words

Repeat stretch.
Oil down the cut.
Twist tight
shape upon shape,
geometry of life.
Comb chaos can cure
disarray into tesselated
masterpiece.
Pity.
Pattern.
Undone doo
gets grips
tight twists
repeating
age-old algorithms.
Equating twirl curls,
bap naps
to undead DNA
multiplexed
onto cabeza
of dark strand storage.
Plopped on the floor
between knees.
Please.
Ouch! Don't…
Ouch!
Headscalpbrainmind
hurts with the calculations

of twine calibrated
centimeter by intricate centimeter
into the extensive
groove soothe
of architectural completion.
Uh oh!
Wait a minute.
Missed one.
Stretch mind's
expansive eye
into how many,
how long,
how artistic,
how,
how,
some white people may ask,
do you do that?
With no answer,
the subdivision
integral
of x
rootedness to infinity
matrices
is done
naturally.

Romare's Potions

Scoop squeeze
Wet earth river bottom
Dark soil secrets
Absorbed roots
Soaked memory
Brown to green bayou
Don't just tell you
Is what the conjur woman said

Bold-breasted robins
Flit and sit
While whole aviaries
Blues cry and jazz juke
Where worms ooze
Rubbed by root
See the pink bird fish
Virgin bleed by the bend
Healed and birthed curing cloths
Is what the conjur woman said

Loud sun covers
Wide walls of bug hum
Framed in vine-wrapped trees
Thick, tall pithy proud
Shroud ground
Greater greens and browns
Warm winds whip and mix
Water sounds
Gurgle drip trickle
Thin blade shimmers
Whisper quiet pipe puffs
Float dove-love-like

Around her magic hair
Clipping time varies
Is what the conjur woman said

Distant trains
Offer call and response
To owl hoots and crow caws
Thicker hands twist grasses into balls
Feel bark for tea
Make honey into mead
Clap chant hymns to roots stems
Leaves seeds and bees
Know the beauty of the flower
Grows with the hour
And so does its power
Sun shifts the day
Hers just gets bolder
When it's colder
Collard greens sweeter
Secreter
When you see her
Burn in full moon light glow
Listen to the land
See the colors and know
Is what the conjur woman said

SUMMER POETRY JAM

Sponsored by the Bridges Programs

HOSTED BY DARRELL "SCIPOET" STOVER

FRIDAY

JUNE 27,1997

6:30 PM

Til Dark

at the

Center for

Documentary Studies

1317 West Pettigrew Street

(off of Swift)

FEATURING ...Raman Soni HOWARD CRAFT Andrea Selch BORN Evon Smith CULVER CLARK ESQUIRE Denise Johnson JAY SULLIVAN JESSIE MCCLAIN Chris Tilley BERNICE REVELLE David Need NKOSI Robert Jeter DAVID ALAN BERKS Asia Feamster MARY YORTY

ALL POETS INVITED FOR OPEN MIC

BRING BLANKETS AND LAWN CHAIRS

Also Featuring...

BRUTHER MONK

VOTED BEST BAND 1996

-INDEPENDENT WEEKLY-

FOR MORE INFORMATION PLEASE CALL JESSIE MCCLAIN AT 660-3678

Bedtime Bugs

Katydids eh eh eh in the distance
while crickets chirp
ear below window's edge.
Silent darkness shimmers in omnipresent sounds,
window screens the only protection.

We speak of love and insects
at the periphery of our dream state
this night bound by sound.
"What color is a katydid?" I ask.
"Black," you say,
as a buzzer screams, "Wrong."
A second guess blurbles out
with assurance,
"Green, green of course."
But crickets are black,
shiny and soulful in their orchestrations.
They could be Basie,
Satchmo or even Nat King Cole
crooning "Nature Boy."
August time into September
milkweed beetles will abound
red and black on green
furry broad milkweed leaves.
They yelp-squeak,
like newborn pups,
for more milk and entomological love.

Papa Bantaba

For Chuck Davis

Ring up Raleigh on 1937 Earth
Get ready to move
Every Kwanzaa Imani January first
'Cause Papa Bantaba arrives anew
He is the go between
Gambia & Senegal
Guinea & Ghana
Kenya & Uganda
Mali & here & there
Between health & healing
He chose
Dance like Sister Pearl Primus on toes
Heart drumming swing daddy of hip
Sky high arms helicopter twist
Igbo go go
Mandiani twitch
Big dude slices through time and space
Motions moons as he ashe' Ashe' ASHE' YO
All over the place
Cascades African culture
Unfurled in tapestries of ritual
Indigo dojo
Dons the heroic garb of griot
Tells our story with feet
Blessed in ancient beat
Sun glide bright
Twirls majestic traditional welcomes
As-salaam-alaikum
All

Everyone of us
Watusi watotos again
Children in the good God space of your presence
Refreshed in the boom of your voice
Every room a dance floor tuned to rejoice

Tall call spirit

        Peace Love Respect

                Peace Love Respect

                        Peace Love Respect

For
    E
      V
        E
          R
            Y
              B
                O
                  D
                    Y
Body body
        Body body
                Body soothed and hugged
By this intercontinental dance collector
Greeted with open doors to ancestry
As umbilical to African diversity
Via your diasporic dance university

Take us back through the passage of no return
Doctor quick wit with the djembe hit
Filled with smile wide pride
Cry joy of Yemanja's vast past
Riding ripples across seas and along riverways
Anacostia, Hudson and Eno
Oshun on the shores of DC, New York City and Durham
Nurtured by the sagest of souls
Olatunji, Holder, Pomare, Sister Johnson Reagon and Dodson
Stop time travel back
As you do that shoulderthang
Ensembles parallel your expressions
As thousands of communities step hand dip
Body nod head bop waist wiggle your lessons
Shekere Blessings
Big Baba of grace
Shimmy poetry kora shake Mandinka taste
Kola nut wedding boogie wave Wolof
Akonting string jam Jola
Riti rock Fula
Take us
Take us into our Brother & Sister lands
Make the happy pappies and magnified mommas glow
At the sight of their workshopped miracles
Moving with Kujichagulia prowess
Fertile visits reap another success
Faith seeds
Each of the bountiful babes of your teaching
Step step
Snap pop
Drop knee
Arm lift
Open palm
Passed on psalms
In your bantaba

Baba

ASANTE ASANTE

ASANTE SANA

Which Anancy are you?

NARRATOR

Which Anancy are you?
Which Anancy?
You know Anancy?
Anancy, the spider.
Anancy, the trickster.
Caribbean "A"-"N"-"A"-"N"-"C"-"Y"
or
Akan, Ghanain, West African "A"-"N"-"A"-"N"-"S"-"I."
Intelligent joker.
Trickster Anancy.
Not trickster as in tacks in the seat of a chair.
(Narrator sits as if in a chair.)
OUCH!!!
(Narrator rises quickly off of imaginary tack.)
But the animal trickster
in communication with us and the spirit world.
The wise and magical.
Anancy, the spider, trickster!

Which Anancy are you?
Bold Anancy of red and black?
(Anancy #1 enters majestically in red and black to front center stage then returns to rear.)
Bright Anancy of sun yellow?
(Anancy #2 enters sprightly in yellow to front center stage then returns to rear.)

Funky Anancy of rich green?
(Anancy #3 enters in green strutting and dancing to front center stage then returns to rear.)
Lovely Anancy of pulsing purple?
(Anancy #4 enters in purple divinely strolling to front center stage then returns to rear.)
Creepy Anancy of eight legs...
(All four move in different directions creepily. Arms up and wrists arched.)
..stalking...
(All hunt in different directions.)
...running...
(All run in different directions.)
...leaping...
(Anancy #1 leaps, then #2 and #4, then #3 and then all simultaneously.)
...pouncing.
(All pounce on imaginary prey and "Screech" or say, "Gotcha.")
Seeing all.
(All look around wide-eyed.)
Knowing all.
(All nod heads and look around in approval.)
Anancy of eight eyes.
(All close their arms in front of their bodies, bow and point heads to audience and rush forward to front stage wiggling their heads.)
Trickster.
(All open arms and stand erect, fists at hips in succession #1, #2, #3 and #4.)
Web spinner of tales...
(All spread out along stage.)

...shooting wondrous words on the wind...
(Upon the word "shooting" all grab hidden cans of Silly String, shake cans and then spray the audience.)
...to win over and over again...
(All back up in unison.)
...jugs of knowledge...
(All line up along back of stage.)
...safety from alligators...
(All spread right leg to the right.)
...hawks...
(All spread left leg to the left.)
...and menacing...
(All hold right arm high closing right fist.)
...monsters.
(All hold left arm up closing left fist.)
Heroic...
(All place fists on hips in bold posture.)
...little Anancy.
(All fold over into balls.)
Ninja spider with the big heart.
(All spring up into mock karate battle postures.)
Ready to challenge...
(Pair off and engage in mock battles.)
...anyone and anything...
(Continue mock battle.)
...with well-placed...
(Stop battle, shake hands and face audience.)
...word webs!
(All shout "Wow" and charge the audience, some leaving stage.)
ANANCY!
(All respond as if called back and return to stage.)
Not ever hurt most times.
(All line up across mid center stage.)
Anancy dusts off
the bumps of day to day battle...

(All dust off knees.)
...the little hurts of name-callers...
(All dust off shoulders, right shoulder with left hand first.)
...the dream destruction of No-No...
(All dust off their foreheads with their right hands.)
...to go on proud and thoughtful...
(All strut around with heads held high with chests out.)
...with freshly gained knowledge...
(All tap their right temples in deep thought.)
...from every lesson learned and story told.
(All run fingers over imaginary pages like they are reading a book held in their left hands.)

Which Anancy?
(All approach front stage and point in different directions, but not at audience.)
Which Anancy?
(All point in another direction, but not at audience.)
Which Anancy are you?
(All point at the audience upon the word "you.")
Bold Anancy of majestic red and black?
(Anancy #1 struts in front and around others who look on jealously. Anancy takes place at the beginning of a line that starts stage right.)
Bright Anancy of sun yellow?
(Anancy #2 glides in front and around others who look on in mouth opened awe.)
Funky Anancy of rich green.
(Anancy #3 shakes and dances around others who shake their heads in disgust.)
Lovely Anancy of pulsing purple?
(Anancy #4 prances around others who turn their heads away as she passes, except #3 who claps and then reaches for Anancy #4 before she takes her place at the end of the line.)
WHICH...
(Each Anancy places hands at hips and spreads legs in bold posture one at a time.)

...ANANCY...

(All hug themselves.)

...ARE...

(All continue hugging.)

...YOU?!!!

(All spread open arms in unison. All start to clap, jump, cheer and give each other high five's as they go off into the audience doing the same to disappear out the back of the theater. Narrator exits stage right.)

THE METAPHYSICS OF MARLEY

second annual birthday celebration of the life and legacy of

Robert Nesta Marley

a tribute in
LECTURE - POETRY - PERFORMANCE

featuring:

DARRELL STOVER
& the SPOKEN WORD
Morton Brooks, Butch Jackson, Sydney March

and the music of
BOB MARLEY and the WAILERS

sunday 2/18/96
221 sheridan street NW
2-6 PM
this event is free
bring a dish and a beverage
for info: (202) 829-4708

Ignancy

For Joani

What's that you say?
He's sufferin' from a bad case of
I-G-N-A-N-C-Y
IGNANCY
That be right
That's how it's spelt
He come up talkin' 'bout
"Gimme some of that"
Then reaches for it with his hands
He dips an empty glass into the champagne
fountain instead of waitin' the long
time it takes for the stuff to
flow into his glass
Brother man cut a fool all the time
Just don't know how to behave himself
No Way No How

Last night at the party
He have to get all loud
Talkin' 'bout
Ohwoo Yeah Ohwoo Yeah Ohwoo Yeah
Clappin' his hands all loud
Had me shoutin' right along with him
Ohwoo Yeah Ohwoo Yeah
Vocalizin' the rap with the little sisters
What's dey name?
Sugar and Spice No Salt and Peppa

He started dancin' all in front of me
Talkin' 'bout
"Come on baby, Let's Dance"
Shakin' his butt
Wigglin' like his backbone was a rubber band
Pumpin' his pelvis
Bendin' at the knees
Arms wavin' in the air
I was thinkin' 'bout how
 Those aerobics classes pay-off on the dance floor
  when the music is getting' down
Then I was thinkin'
  'bout that brother and me dancin' Woo
If my momma saw me she would say
 "Get it girl"
  'cause she suffers from the same
   IGNANCY that my dance partner
    and even I am infected with
I remember the adults gatherin' around
 clappin' and shoutin' when we were little
 doin' our versions of the latest
   dances in the middle of the living room
    after a big family dinner
Uncle Mike joinin' us on the dance floor
Showin' us his particular style of IGNANCY

Yeah, me a loud boisterous woman
An actress who loves havin' a good time
Shoutin' out my vivaciousness
I ain't worried 'bout my IGNANCY showing
I am comfortable in my exhibitions and exclamations
In fact I'm ready to cut up again
"You wanna dance?"
        OHWOO YEAH

Stepped It Up and Gone On

Durham City Marker Commemoration, June 16, 2001
for Blind Boy Fuller on the American Tobacco Trail

Hayti Hayti Handed down
Handed down
Hayti Hayti Handed down
Rev. Gary Davis
Told this man
to tell Brownie McGee
to hook up with Sonny Terry
'cause there's some dancin' to be done
some 'baca to be sold
some stories to be told
by a string singin'
git pickin'
Blind, Bad
Durham dude
Wadesboro
        BOY
WHIPPIN' WICKEDLY
WONDERFUL LICKS
LIKE BLACK LEAGUES
OF SOUTHERN STRUGGLIN'
LOOKIN' FOR LOVE
IN ALL THE WRONG PLACES
RECORDIN' BOOCOO
HISTORY
TELL TELLIN'
SPIDER MAN
ON THE STRINGS
LOOKIN' LIKE MY GRANDADDY

UP FROM THE CAROLINAS
FULTON HIM MACK DADDY
SLICK DAPPER
DAN GENIUS
CLEAR SEEIN' THIRD EYE
PREACHIN' PARTY PARTY
MAN CHILD
PLAYIN' NATIONAL STEEL
IN A COTTON RAG LAND
HAYTI HAYTI HANDED DOWN…

The Institute for Critical U.S. Studies presents

NEW ØRLEANS MUSIC IN EXILE

a documentary by Robert Mugge

Please join Mark Anthony Neal, Associate Professor of African and African American Studies, and Darrell Stover, Cultural Historian and Poet, for dinner and a movie, followed by conversation about Hurricane Katrina's continued impact on culture and community.

Rebirth Brass Band in Houston

Tuesday March 27th
7:30-10:00pm
Mary Lou Williams Center
201 West Union Building

visit the Critical U.S. Studies website:
http://www.jhfc.duke.edu/icuss

In Duke's D.C.

Brother Was Jazz wink his eye
and the cymbals would splash
accent notes for a Satin Doll.
Brother Was Jazz yawn
and the horn section would waw waw
up into cool havens where angels dwell.
Brother Was Jazz snap his fingers
a couple of times and the bass would bottom
the cha cha-ed percussion. Uh huh!
Brother Was Jazz tap his foot
as he pulled his ear
and the piano would tinkle a little bit.
Brother Was Jazz burp and y'all would say,
"Now son you know better,"
as the orchestra changed the beat
from soul screams to soft baby cries.
Yeah, when Brother Was Jazz flies
he swoops through Howard Theater,
Lincoln Collonade, Turner's Arena,
the D.C. Armory and on your radio - LIVE!
After a whirlwind world tour
Brother Was Jazz hits rest notes
at Ward Place Northwest.
Brother is jazz,
always was and will be
with us here in Duke's D.C.

Prayer Blues for Brother Otis

We nod now teary
to the scorching glow ascending
from the bottom of bones
as the Mississippi shimmers
lively ripples of you.
Who you are.
Why you ululate
Uhuru Muntu Nommo Mojo
movements in the complex keys of us.
All simplified in your gaze.

Baobab. Oak. High-John.
Deep root oozes you
and you ooze it.

Graybeard was no ghost or rogue.
You, Graybeard, the magic man,
traveling the rails,
a migration twisted and stretched
through a billion billion songs of hurt,
laughing craziness out
and love in.
Some stolen.
Creator calling you now,
vessel of life's juice poured full,
mythic your wanderings and wisdom.
Were you in the cotton patch burning bush,
back on some ship
taken over by you,
fighting
upon the arrival of they to your shores?
War gospel sung at each defeat and victory.

Proud heir to the unknown reaches
of our beginnings and endings.
Deacons defer all judgements to you.
Funky scat solos
countertime music maker.
Gabriel's horn holds counsel
in the jowls of your boom.
Over here in the corner of the juke,
where bluesmen swap drinks and tales,
I hear only the remarkable missions
you have been sent on
in many disguises.
Thunder and lightening blaze you.
Tidal waves roar you.
Twister wild you.

Soul Soldier. Solitude Spirit. Sojourn Soarer.
Say, you told us about it
as you pointed
with a fist of black iron
as greeting and passing blessing.

Nurturer,
none of your flock
ever unprotected.
Bathed in your voicings,
anointed in your teachings,
only dancing to your wave,
jumping to your beat,
hands raised to your testimony.

Ask Tupac: Ethnopoetics of The Hood

Rapper recorded on the wind now.
Electric blue verbs
heard in any school,
on any bus,
through any means
are calling us.
Put your ear to the asphalt.
Let me run a line.
Don't get stuck up,
pistol-whipped by the science.
A lot of bloods bleed
each time they open their mouths.
They spit red rhymes
so full of soul fire
you flazed in the meanings,
Ralph Ellison's,
Terry McMillan's,
every one.

Their oral cadence has you
all funked up.
Images of the avenging slave,
mad Black man,
drug dealer
wanting all your toys,
pulls a million triggers
to blast the myth.
The rage still backfires
on many city streets.
Lemmings over the edge
hit the hard rocks of America
with beckoning cries of final resolution,

screams of defiant retribution,
breaking news from the underground.

Dude got shot.
You don't know
if he's dead or not.
Could be just a vaccination,
rite of passage,
believed to be the latest thing
in soular transmutation,
some jive eschatology.
Ask Tupac.
He died for the sins of Hip Hop.
Love and moral decay
boasted through
busted 40 ounces
and other strange brews.
He covered the waterfront.
Got wet too often
along some parts of the shore.

In the book of rap
there's always more to the phrase.
Each line not a sentence
but a paragraph
in the greater book of Nommo.

Tupac's book is complete.
Case closed.
He had to go.
He no different
than any of us
children of the Blues:
Jesus,
Crispus Attucks, Malcolm X,
Henry Dumas, Jimi Hendrix,
Peter Tosh, Len Bias,

Etheridge Knight...
Brothers have been dying
for the sins of man,
on the humble,
over the wrong woman,
in the wrong wars,
doing no wrong
for ages.
A new language is neccesary
to make sense of it all
and meeting at the crossroads
still works.

Ask Tupac.
He sold his soul
for the sins of Hip Hop,
for the messages wrapped
in the badder than bad
street sounds of the dozens
and the ancestral sex of juke joints.
Distant.
Gone.

Any number of rap boppers
with viper tongues
could run it down.
The old school of the street,
sewer hole of rhyme-crime,
speaks clearly
through the blood of the slaughtered.
Rob a man
with his pants down
and he can't run away.

Viciousness of the wild,
territoriality of the plain,
geopolitics of war,

national security
always come to our corners.
The answers come
in stranger ways though.
Sometimes as questions.
If one pants leg up
means I'm selling
and another pants leg up
means I'm buying,
then what does both legs up
with my pants hanging down mean?
If you ain't got no father
and you ain't got no mother
can't we find someone for you
other than the latest CIA crack daddy?

Who's gonna put the period on the end
of the poem with no end
that only contains these lines -
"Nobody saved the Titanic,
but Shine did save his own
Black ass?"
Ask Tupac.
He had a death wish
the likes of which
Charles Bronson had never seen.

A baby screams for attention,
so do rappers.
What should we really scream for?
40 acres and a mule?
Two dogs and a BMW?
Endless chickens and justice?
Ask Tupac.
He died in a vain attempt
to save Hip Hop from itself.

The Lord saves,
not the preacher,
if you take the right
precautions and proactions.
Inspired,
rappers like preachers
are the ritual revealers
of the unknown.
Ask Tupac.
He died
to get some answers for Hip Hop.

Thug,
trapped rat
fighting back,
just gave up on life.
Round my old way
they like Tupac,
dying
to see if they serve Alize
in heaven.

THE SPOKEN WORD

Presents

A Series of Readings and Discussions
followed by
An Open Reading
featuring
Local Writers
at

KOBOS

2441 18th Street, NW
Washington, DC

— One Sunday A Month at 4:00 PM —

- **Sunday, October 21, 1990 — Lasana Mack & Rabia Rayford**
  [David Walker first attacked slavery]
- **Sunday, November 18, 1990 — Kenny Carroll and Jennifer Smith**
  [November 15, 218 BC, Hannibal crossed the Alps]
- **Sunday, December 23, 1990 — Leslie Lewis and Darrell Stover**
  [Chancellor Williams born December 22, 1898 in Bennetteville, SC
  Cheik Anta Diop born December 29, 1923 in Diourbel, Senegal]
- **Sunday, January 18, 1991 — Venus Thrash and Larry Ferguson**
  [Osei Bansu, Ashanti leader, defeats the British at Assamke, Ashanti]
- **Sunday, February 17, 1991 — Akindele Akinde and Patricia Elam-Ruff**
  [Frederick Douglas born February 14, 1817 in Tuckahoe, Maryland]
- **Sunday, March 17, 1991 — John Trammell and Judy Cohall**
  [Zensi Miriam Makeba born March 4, 1932 in Prospect Township, South Africa
  Harriet Tubman died on March 10, 1913]

For more information
(202) 332-9580

Land, Love Loss

for the Gullah and Piedmont Carolinas

Searing summer lessons
of unpaid toil told
through cotton sweat,
tobacco tears
and red rice blood.
Green marsh,
tidal washed wealth,
like fertile earth
yields enough for all.
No real dollars,
just bitter harvests
for the tenders,
tenants
and mud-soaked
blessed.

Long water run
out the eyes
through the land
to the sea,
acres of gated waterfront
once fished by me.
Rusting tractors
and repossessed wishes
cast in post-Reconstruction
and Jim Crowed screams.
They take,
take,
take.

Where you come from,
palmettos and pines,
ain't always gonna be there
if you forget it.
Hidden under resorts
and in the hands
of loan sharks
disguised in white
under white,
clans of agricultural locals
and coastal
carpetbaggers.
They take,
take,
take.

It's OK
to tenant cook
at the BBQed Shrimp,
fold linen
at the Plantation
Reconstruction Rescinded Estates,
and stay
at tenth of an acre,
vinyl hut inn.
No visible spot
on the water board
or soybean subsidy,
tobacco quota committee.
Expect no change
from the toll bridge
that glides
over your land.
They take,
take,
take.

"40 acres and a what!
How about this choice
red dirt,
all you want
on a year to year lease.
I'll keep the books
and half
from the next ten summers.
Oh, by the way,
I got a nice store,
everything you need.
You can get it all
on cotton pickin' credit."
They take,
take,
take.
First tenants
long disappeared
according to the bureau
of ethnic cleansing.
Second tenants
cheated and disgraced,
now told to wait.
Third tenants
arrive daily,
kiss the land
after the border,
harsh dreams waiting.
They take,
take,
take.
Septima Clark shouts,
"educate yourself."
Cesar Chavez dice,
"libre la tierra
y la gente."

Robert Williams instructs,
"arm yourself against racists."
Now let them try
as tired of it
Mother Earth
takes,
takes,
takes
back.

I Remember the Rubberman of Negril

It's these tears that I can't hold inside
Balloon's air wants to flow out
but the skin holds it in
and not my eyes alone can control these emotions
The people believe in 'One Love'
I chose to believe what I felt
and thinking back upon it
the people were rich as the land
Spirits tropical nutrient fortified
Green, lush life-loving vegetation
Clear, fresh full-feeling air
Blue, scintillating soul-soothing waters
and the Rubberman's smile
'Yah, mahn!'
'We get motorbikes!'
'I take you and de lady to the mountains where
I and I see where the Arawak nation lived in the caves!'

He came up on us not as some beach bum
but as some washed up treasure
carried by peaceful waves
A career of contortion balanced by concentration
Etched in that smile revealing a life of performance
Babies in chairs carried on chins
Held in air by thin wires of yogi magic
Ragamuffin mind degreed in common sense study
A country wit that kept our honeymoon IRIE
He, an unofficial tour guide, and we, blessed in his presence,
shared molasses bread
below the ackee fruit trees filled with parrots
as he sketched our next adventure

The Rubberman knows his people's needs
His people love him in return
relishing his every arrival
as if he was returning from the hunt
bearing provisions for a long winter
But here in Jamaica, no long winters
Only daily struggle against IMF inquisitors
Softened by tourism's tricklings and the land's blessings
I remember the Rubberman now
like the passing of Bob Marley
It's these tears I can't hold inside

RUN ON WATER

An examination of coastal Carolina's natural and human history through the African American experience during the Civil War, focusing on the role and actions of US Colored Troop Regiments.

Special Guest Historian

C. R. Gibbs

Author of "Black, Copper and Bright: The District of Columbia Black Civil War Regiment"

Saturday, May 22, 2004

2:00 PM

St. Joseph's Performance Hall
Hayti Heritage Center
804 Old Fayetteville Street
Durham

FREE TO THE PUBLIC

LECTURE, POETRY AND SLIDE PRESENTATION

Featured artists and performances by Jackie Marriott, Thomasi McDonald, percussionist Morton Brooks and moderator/panelist and researcher of the project Darrell Stover and his son, Darius Stover.

The Run On Water Project aired on WNCU 90.7 and several coastal stations during the month of February and March 2004 as 13-2.5 minute radio vignettes. These vignettes featured poetry, narratives and interviews with scholars of note in antebellum and civil war period North Carolina.

This program was funded by the North Carolina Humanities Council, the St. Joseph's Historic Foundation, and WNCU 90.7

FOR MORE INFORMATION CALL 683-1709
OR WWW.HAYTI.ORG

For My Grandfather Said

"Who dat said who dat when I said who dat?"
Is what he said
as he creeped into the apartment
like the bogeyman into our dreams
as we spent the night at our grandparents'
those many weekends.
"Who dat said who dat when I said who dat?"
echoed up the staircase
from down below with
"I'm on the second step."
Him comin' to get us
maybe 'cause like grandma said,
"Y'all pay one way or another
for that candy you snuck before dinner."
"Who dat said who dat when I said who dat?"
Our grandfather on our father's side
stood tall and ancient,
dark and deep
like North Carolina country roads at night.
He was full of games and stories
like the plenitude of cookies and candies
in grandma's pantry.
Beat you everytime at checkers
except when he knew
you needed some encouragement.
"Who dat said who dat when I said who dat?"
Stories that leave you seeing things at night
that only the covers or a pillow
over your head
could protect you from.
If you couldn't see it

it couldn't see you.
"Who dat said who dat when I said who dat?"
Gardenin' man
set things to growin' right
so that by the time grandma came along
all she had to do was say, "Jump,"
and them ripe and ready to eat
beans and tomatoes
would hop into her apron.
Speakin' of jumpin'.
He could jump boogie,
hand clap,
shimmy shuffle shoe
better than the best.
"Who dat said who dat when I said who dat?"

Hard workin' hand man
gestures silently with fingers
talkin' loud
like history
pourin' from the mind of John Henrik Clark.
In this they were alike
for they could stand facin' each other
on either side of the mirror
reflectin' Angola,
the Congo
and an Akan priestliness.
"Who dat said who dat when I said who dat?"
He was the blue black brother,
blue crystals for eyes,
gray crowned,

heart and soul of the land,
earthen brown.
"Who dat said who dat when I said who dat?"
Of him,
my beans,
greens,
tomatoes,
peppers,
cantaloupe,
brussel sprouts,
broccoli
and cabbage
growin' daddy would say,
"He's steeped in the blues-gospel,"
gospel-blues voicings,
echoed in the way
Thomas A. Dorsey would say,
"You've got to change a little."
"Who dat said who dat when I said who dat?"
is what my grandfather said to me
and dis is what I said of him!
"Who dat said who dat when I said who dat?"
"Who dat said who dat when I said who dat?"
"Who dat said who dat
when I said
WHO DAT!?"

Culture vs Computers

Ain't no technodude gonna feed the hungry
Ain't no technoslacker gonna save the children
Ain"t no technocolor gonna improve the image
that was clearly seen in black and white
But now fades to grey, fuzzy snow
Statically imitating death dying
786,432 pixels strong
Nothing writes the epitaph of an electronic
information overloaded landscape better than
a blank, little screen punched in by a book of
Zora Neale Hurston's HooDooin' fiction
Now creatin' a VooDooin' nonvirtual reality
Suckin' juice from the sorry souls of techmongers
Freein' the people from ATM futures and PC slavery
Workin' their own strange God magic
Puttin' brain food on the table
A slicin' spirit back in their hearts
And bill worries behind them
for their credit histories
caught a bad case of erasure
Memory blank out fade out
Replaced by dancin' black digits
Positive numbers lookin' like they win lottos
Everyday
War babies resisting electronic spankings
Hip hoppin' to the radio
Where all you hear is Black Martial Music
on every station of the FM band
Autodigitally programmed
Good to go Go-Go
ALL JAZZ ALL BLUES NO NEWS

No COMMERCIALS
No ads or subtractions
No irritating mouths distractin'
Just AcousticSoulfulBebopBooms
Music accompanying the question
"Did you read the warning in the Terminator's eyes?"

What the Fingers Do

for Gypsy at Talk of the Town

The Blind Brothers Blake,
Lemon Jefferson
and Boy Fuller
in their turn had mojo hands,
extended thumbs
that passed for bass,
drum and press.
Grip the tools you use
and deny the animal in you,
deny desire except in mating time.
Can an octopus play the piano?
Its flesh too soft, you say.
But its tentacles do grip and caress.
Wrap you in a watery swirl of love.
The bluesman knows all about it.
Lute charmers Peetie Wheatstraw,
Muddy Waters, John Lee Hooker
and Elmore James
handed it down.
Fingers create drama,
create travelogues dipped in song.
Fingers wiggle as fancy dancers
in romance with deadly curves
that echo every touch.
Slide down the chords of gut.
Squeeze some funky stuff
into howls of how good it is.
Rub and strum
until the neighbors knock

and the police come.
Another town doesn't want you
no more.
Time to engage thumb to the wind.
John Hurt, Robert Johnson
and Archie Edwards drive by
as you grab your honey
and throw her over your back.
In the next town,
fingers at play,
she'll understand.

"Got that Touch" Cats

for generations of Baltimore and North Carolina jazz, 8/30/03 at Capper's with Yusef Salim on piano, Freeman Ledbetter on bass, Adia Ledbetter and Vernon Wolts on vocals, Oscar Wright on guitar, Whit Williams on sax, Chuck Leonard on drums and Hubert "Count" Hayes on everything

Used to be midnight
lasted all night,
last call didn't call, y'all.
Used to be alto Vernon on vocals
stirring deep blue Maryland mornings.
Whit Williams big band blew
boppers show stoppers
of standard time love
like many up-from-Carolina cats.

Groove down time now,
50th Raleigh reunion revels in
master music mentors as counts.
"How do you do that?"
Mentor asks student
who used to ask,
"How do you do that?"
Followed by 3 years
woodsheddin' round about midnight.

"I knew you
when you were like that."
A parallel palm
measures magic
of time, height and meter.

"You ain't 55."
A student's excitement
still brightens the room,
heart of the teacher,
like the blue in green
to yellow in orange
to hot red fire
of an ancient alchemist's
secret night laboratory.
"I feel like I'm 26,"
Chuck of the master brushes says
kneeling in the presence
of the mystical sage, Count.
One-two, one, two, three, four.

Piano catches up
20 years later
with the Arthur Prysock
voice of Vernon,
a time and space shift gift
like Nina Simone in Tryon,
Baltimore and Paris
all at once.
Check the triangulation, baby!
Playing changes
to displace relativity,
Cool Joe Yusef,
so full of love,
so full of the planet,
community.
Scholar of inspiration
encouraged learnin' the beat
as soft voice floatin'
under the melody
keepin' the prettiest feather
in midair

where we can see it,
understand it
as mathematical sound miracles.
Everybody
to him a sister or brother
of everybody else
as they feel whispers,
see changes,
applaud solos,
Earth beings
with touched souls,
him being in the now-and-then,
timer of the tinkle keys,
dabbler in the unification of spirits,
one, two, three hundred or more at a time.

Buster Brown had a baby at 75,
singing young at 96
like the spirit of the drummer
who gots the touch
on skin,
on tang splash cymbals,
on his tight bass,
not boom boom
attack funk fake and fade,
but serious, continuous funk
foot dynamics snap,
keep it happening,
timed pocket poking,
knowing them tunes
'cause Count told you,
"Do your homework,
woodshed!"

"Count,
wizard of the whisper brushes,

he cool.
No,
that man
that man
IS HIP!"
Count, slick and tight,
kept magic
every day and night.
13 year old watched,
asked, "How you do that?"
3 years woodsheddin'.
Disappeared.
10 years later,
not so little Chuck returned.
Count asked, "Where you been?"
"I been with the Four Tops."
"Brush-work got me the gig!"
"Got that from Count."
"Got that from Count"
"...from Count...from Count...from Count."
Five-five, four-four on three.

The Literature Division Of The D.C. Public Library
And
The American Poetry And Literacy Project
Present

A PROGRAM PARTIALLY FUNDED BY THE HUMANITIES COUNCIL OF WASHINGTON, D.C.

GREAT AFRICAN AMERICAN POETS

A READING AND DISCUSSION FROM

THE BLACK POETS

An Anthology By Dudley Randall

Presented By

DARRELL STOVER

Folk Poems, Spirituals, Performance Poetry, Including The Works Of Langston Hughes, Lucille Clifton, Amiri Baraka, Gwendolyn Brooks, Countee Cullen, Paul Laurence Dunbar, Nikki Giovanni And More!

Wednesday * April 24, 1996 * 12:00 noon

Martin Luther King Memorial Library
901 G Street, NW * Main Lobby

For More Information, Call (202) 727-1281

Free Copies Of THE BLACK POETS Will Be Distributed By The American Poetry And Literacy Project After The Program.

Woman Blues

1.
Blues Holiday Horned in on Bessie, Mama
Lady feels on in my/your mind
It's been hard. I mean bad baby
I/You/All of Us need something, really, 'cause all
we got right now is strange fruit
"I lost a good woman and a good woman done lost me" blues.

2.
The old, old-wisened Brother on the stage
In the discussion group said,
"Sisters, I mean all of you, I got something to tell you."
"I, along with the rest of the Brothers want to thank you
For putting up with us these past 200-400 years."
As we all clapped I almost cried.

3.

A.

Celestial purple - a color of thought, a book, a movie
I saw with my Elders and I saw you.
Saved seats in SOCY 105 back in '75
A first time University of Muppet crush
Ain't talk to you in 10 years isn't it?
Wow - married and a daughter
That 1st stuff I wrote to you if you still got any of it, don't sell it yet
Let me try to make a few coins off what I'm writing lately.

B.

Verandas for viewing youth and youthfulness
again and again
Ambergris washed up on high hope shores
What went wrong in the waters could have only been just play

But I saw your wrist bloody disappear into slits
Goodbyes drowned by "for sisters only" passion.

C.

How to make the heart of a butterfly whose battered wings
  have got it through to a December in which azaleas now bloom
How to make better its soul
which has been blown by ancient winds
  Winds which blew it to me only to blow it away
How to make better verses
without competin' with your innervisions
How to make better your absence
unemployed writing without you
How to create a more beautiful Buddha
when that Buddha embodies all Beauty
How to make better
  to make better
    make better
      better.

4.
Sex
An evil word in the context of what people do to get it
What men, boys, fathers, uncles, brothers, cousins have done
Sisters unitin' will change all that
What men, boys, fathers, uncles, brothers,
cousins haven't done
Sisters unitin' 2x4's to the head, greasy grits to the back
Wise words to the mind and love to the heart
will change all that
Young man, woman-chasin', heart-breakin',
havin' to face responsibility

Growin' up, your true honey leavin'
will change all that.

5.
If it wasn't another man might have been another woman
Might have been that mark that gave the impression
That that shirt had been stabbed 'til it bled lipstick
Yeah, it might have been another woman
Another woman who thought she had a good man
Gonna go through some funky times to keep that man
End up losin' him and herself
'Cause some other jazzier model
with deadlier lipstick will come along
"Don't call me no more
and I especially won't call you when you're married."
Just leave me in these in-between times tearful with those
"I lost a good woman and a good woman done lost me" blues.

Sister DANCE

for Pearl E. Primus at the Smithsonian 2-2-90

I. Your credo echoes in the limbs of lithely spirits
whose motions mandate the power of movement
Movement rhyming with rhythms
All sounds of ancient ritual passed down through
the ages over and over again forever African
Foot to Earth connects communication link to sky
to ancestors who nod in approval
of a people's cultural imperative
We Dance for Life!
We Dance for Those Who've Gone Before!
We Dance!

II. You share images of a legacy
"Tell me of my people"
You speak to the truer nature of your art/our art
Tell me of my people"
You, who have reconnected the umbilical cord
to our brothers and sisters across the creek
to bring ceremonial flights of fertility, rites of passage,
and war against evil
"Tell me of my people"
Sister DANCE
Tell me

III. Sister DANCE, not telling you, but
acknowledging that you are DANCE
Look at you in air stopping time
in performance after performance
You have discovered the elixir of longevity

Look at you on the screen on the tip of your toe
capturing the movement in Langston's poem
"A Negro Speaks of Rivers" that energizes
Our travels down the many rivers of time
Rivers of whip scars
Rivers of blood
Rivers of sharks, death, and struggle
You, who danced across the Middle Passage and back
The Jesus/Moses of Black Dance
Grace us with your experiences
Dancing amongst the Watusi and Fanga
Diasporan Dance Mother
You embody the lexicon of African choreography

IV. A proclamation for Pearl E. Primus Day in this nation's capital
A proclamation in recognition of a Dance Warrior
A proclamation of a Black Art battle won
You have challenged all disbelief in your spirit
You went from aspirations of doctor to student of dance
to afrocentric anthropologist to become the essential healer
Knowing us and our true needs
Engaging in a social conquest that catapults our insights
into that ultimate freedom – DANCE

V. You teach the controlling of time and space
Your interpretation of our cultural texts
puts life abundant in these tomes
Strange fruit has been reaped but through your redefining
the Polyrhymic Us becomes central again
Blossoms sending sweet aromas
Updated fruit plucked from a nurturing vine

VI. Sister DANCE
Sister DANCE
We Shall Dwell
In Your Spirit
Full of Ourselves
And What It Means
To be Black and Gifted
Aware of the African in Us
And Whenever/Wherever We Boogie
We Will Move to the Rhythms
You Have Taught Us
Sister DANCE.

Witness at the Center of the Fire Funnel

for Pharoah Sanders

I saw the sunrise with black neon flashing
"Pharoah"
"Pharoah"
"Pharoah"
all on its surface.
A wailing that had always been there
rose in volume like screaming cats in heat.
Tornadoes looped all around
with the sound of chants for black spirits
taking over the airwaves.
There was no station,
TV, radio, cable or short-wave,
that didn't carry that repetitious poetry
accompanied by mbira.
"Pharoah blows forever,
powering the sunshine,
scattering hot light
into desirous souls."
"Pharoah Blows Forever,
Powering The Sunshine,
Scattering Hot Light
Into Desirous Souls."
"PHAROAH BLOWS FOREVER,
POWERING THE SUNSHINE,
SCATTERING HOT LIGHT
INTO DESIROUS SOULS."
The stars twinkle in the night

'cause Pharoah's horn told them to.
Pharoah's sax worm-holed him
to distant spaces
where there was nothing
but beautiful darkness
and in that solitude
he blew up spirals of twinkling light,
galaxies on a universal journey.
A short little wild man of blessed muse
with eyes that saw all said,
"Come back Pharoah."
"Come Back Pharoah."
"COME BACK PHAROAH."
The chant went out
over all the airwaves
and down he came
in the shimmering rain,
each drop splattering sound.
Agogo bells,
tambourine rattles and shakes,
conga beats and pianissimo
registers high up in our hearts.
The wetness combined in a flow
that Pharoah rode,
sax directed each and every ripple.
Periodic bubbles pop,
release seeds
fertile as any Earth mother.

Sprouting genetic memory,
chants of creation,
chants of distant knowledge,
chants of God's desire
remind the soul of every cell
of its connection with every other
in each and every living,
dead and gone thing
as the planets' unify in orbit
around their suns,
as this and other galaxies
travel light years on.
Pharoah's sax opens the conduit
for the Creator to burn his desire on it all.
That little Baraka man screams
again and again,
"Come back Pharoah."
"Come Back Pharoah."
"COME BACK PHAROAH."
And Pharoah sends back his soul
in a prayer chanted in many tongues.
"I ain't gone no where,
but in every corner
I am there where
my heart hangs at the mouth of any sax
and goes out any time they blow.
Soul! Soul! Soul!
You got Soul!"
Soular essence of life
sounds like a sax wail
in the wee hours of creation
when nothing but waking birds peep
and crickets peacechirp.
A soft Pharoah-guided sax cry
provides the energy for the planet
to open its eyes again this morning

with a yawn of spring air.
A sadness comes over us
like the passing of a cloud
before the sun.
We freeze in a flute romp
whispered in one of Pharoah's quieter moments.
Then out comes the sun
as Pharoah picks up his ax
and blows us love.

The North Carolina A&T State University Creative Writing Program Presents:

The Carolina on My Mind Reading Series

***Celebrating the special edition of the** Obsidian Journal (Aforebo: A Harvest of North Carolina Writers of African Descent).*

The Creative Writing Program welcomes you to an historic evening with the best of North Carolina's Black poets writing and performing in the genre today. The quilting of their voices recalls the mighty stream of African American voices from the earliest periods through the ensuing decades. Come out and be inspired, uplifted and sustained by the collective artistry of their words and wisdoms. Stick around to chat and for the authors book signing to follow.

Featuring: ***Darrell Stover * Grace Ocasio * Carolyn Beard Whitlow * L. Teresa Church * Lenard D. Moore * Gideon Young * Ojaide, Tanure * Crystal Smith * L. Lamar Wilson * Sheila Smith McKoy * Anjail Rashida Ahmad***

****This program is free and open to the public****

~A joint project with *Obsidian Journal's* Sheila Smith McKoy, Editor (North Carolina State University) and special edition editor Lenard D. Moore of The African American Writers' Collective.

When: The evening of Wednesday, November 9, 2011.
Time: Doors open at 6:30 pm; program start: 7:00 pm.
Location: Auditorium A218 (second floor), General Classroom Building (Corners of N. Benbo and Sullivan Roads). Parking: Parking Lot G-1 on N. Benbow Road side and at Aggie Stadium.

For more information contact: Dr. Anjail Rashida Ahmad, E-mail: arahmad@ncat.edu, Tel: 336.334.7771, ext. 2370.

The Creative Writing Program: "Leading with Service – Motivating through Words and Ideas"

Coltrane Poem

Want to write me a Coltrane Poem
A poem that hits stars
Shattering into rains
Of sound coming
Down all around
Shouts, screams
Bebop yells
Bohemian
Black
Blows BEYOND

Want to write us a Coltrane poem
A poem snatching hearts
Into a Love Supreme
Cooperative
Collective of
Our favorite things
Chillin'
Absolute Cool
Profound Cool
Out there

Want to write Coltrane a Coltrane poem
A poem sending thank you's
To you whenever wherever
You are played in brain
In the great on and on
Take us

Electronic Control

Metro Lover swerves in and out of the Metronet. Somewhere along the Red Line he dips into a tunnel. Up ahead the metaphysical reality of the Metro electronic works starts to funnel. The schismatrix passage tightens an arcing and pulsing lightening bolt around Metro Lover's true and only escape hole.

Suddenly, a piece of viral infiltration quickly flutters into the passage in front of him. Metro Lover blinks as the passage goes to nothingness along with the no longer present retroviral infophage. He blinks again just as the 'closed shut' opens in front of his face. With his eyes shut, he passes through.

Why was he not fazed? He could have been flazed to the "Zone of Zero Funkativity." Imagine that, a place with no funk. Tsk. Tsk. Tsk. He knew that he was down with "The All of It" and it was all about being on the One. He taps into it everyday. He's got no choice. His neurospiritual matrix is permeated by it. If it dies, he dies and vice versa. His essential symbiosis and reason for living has everything to do with protecting and serving "The All of It."

Just now he uses it to zip through to the Green Line Anacostia/Alexandria electronet just beyond the grasp of doom where OoLaLaLa asks, "What took you so long?" Just as the thunder lightening 'dice your sorry butt up' zipspits to the "Zone of Zero Funkativity" the holographed wimpunk hooligans that were on his tale trying to bring an end to this story. Wimpunk hooligan programs sent on his trail by netware corporate control freaks who can't stand his world/universe/"The All of It" saving feats are an exponentially increasing danger.

Metro Lover arcs a neon blaze of green, red, and yellow permanent, glow-in-the-dark, shine-bright-in-the-sunshine cyberslime on the wall where the Metro exits the tunnel to cross the Potomac River into Virginia from L'Enfant Plaza station with his rumor killing signature "METRO LOVER LIVES AS DOES OOLALALA!!!," just another love splirt delivered by Metro Lover's unseen hand from the sizzling hot third rail of the Metro network. Black exclamation points top it all off as Metro Lover blows his finger tips and holsters his virtual remote control, wholistic jazz blaring in the background.

If you have any questions ask ASC - the Anacostia Science Club - found somewhere in the deep southeast corner of DC. If you got any answers get in touch through e-mailing Azalea@TakomaPark.Badbabe when the moon is full. Next thing you know you'll be meeting Azalea at the Takoma Park Metro station platform above the third rail with a band of mocking bird watchers.

Their ultimate test of faith in "The All of It" is to release Metro Lover and OoLaLaLa from the computer works wonderland of the Metro electronet where they are trapped. But not for long as the mockingbird sings in tune to the simultaneous orgasm music of OoLaLaLa and Metro Lover. Their release is complete at the third rail clasp party at midnight as the mockingbird, watchers and all whistle "Get Up for the Down Stroke Everybody Get Up!"

And the globalnet control freaks will really go spastic with fear then. Their nomadic neocolonial control of the electroverse cloaked in hidden hand divisiveness will be greatly jeopardized when Metro Lover and OoLaLaLa are freed.

Is The Beat

for Max Roach

Tit Titit Tit Tit Tit Titit
Tit Titit Tit Tit Tit Titit
Tit Titit Tit Tit Tit Titit
Is the Beat North Carolina born
        Where deep love and life
            Carries us into the struggle
Is the Beat holy roller tambourines
        And trap set gospel
            Celebratin' a groovy God
Is the Beat Bed-Stuy settlement
        Standard Time
            Where Spike Lee established
                Not a renaissance
                    But a continuation
Is the Beat where ever
you have summoned sticks
        unto animal skin
            tight, taut Tang Tang Bop
Is the Beat back
        Damn near some 60 odd years
            Where you changed the tone
Tang Tang Bop Boom Tch Tch Tch
Jamming with Bird, Prez, Diz
Coleman Hawkins, Clifford Brown
            Monk
Sonny Rollins, Kenny Dorham
Booker Little, Ramsey Lewis
            Abbey Lincoln
Need I name on?

Jammin' Jazz
Jammin' something new
Jammin' Us
Is the Beat incessantly insisted
Freedom Now! March Time! Freedom Now!
ddDoomp ddDoomp
ddDoomp Doomp Doomp
Tit Titit Tit Tit Tit Titit
Tit Titit Tit Tit Tit Titit
Tit Titit Tit Tit Tit Titit
Tattap!
Is the beat
Love letters
Smoothed by whispering brushes
Sending touch
Sending feel,
Sending melodic Tch Tch Tch
Cymbals maintaining the pace
Cymbals establishing the go
Go between hearts
Emotional networks
Tang Tang Tch Tang Tang Tch Tch
Hi-hat splash
Is the Beat
Ice Ice Baby Cool
Is the Beat MBOOM MBOOM M-BOOOOM
Is the Beat Onomatopoeia Onomatopoeia ONOMATOPOEIA
Formation of Words Words Words
Imitating Sounds

Percussive Sounds Bang Tch Bop
Is the Beat you
Is the Beat Philly Joe Jones heard
Is the Beat learned or in us all the time?
Is the Beat Max
Is the Beat Roach
Is the Beat collective Bang
Collective Orchestrative Doom Boom to soothe to heal to heat
Heat! HEAT! HEAEAEAT!
Chime In Bang Drum Doom Boom Doom
Boom Boom
Is the Beat Max Roach
With Us Hush hush!
I Still Hear It
Building
Is the Beat direction
Leaders
Where are the leaders?
The leaders are in the making
In the drumming, coming on strong
Bangin' Bashin' Forced Sound
Is the Beat
Is the Beat Max You, Yes You You Max
T-Tch T-Tch T-Tch T-Tch
Bash Bang Bop Tch Maaaaa
aaaaaa
aaaaaax!
Beat as mean as you wanna!

WASHINGTON, DC 2009 INAUGURAL WEEKEND HOUSE PARTY

Clave for Son

For Darius on Father's Day

Ring Rattle the Beginning
Ring Rattle the Flow
Ring Rattle the Destiny
The Destiny of Sons
Ring Rattle of Boy Talk
Warrior Wails
Ring the Sabers
The Spirit of Hard Blazing Metal
Lest We Forget the Priviledge We Have in Sons
Sons to Raise
Ring Rattle the Joy of the Village
New Seed on Earth
This Bantaban
Ring Rattle to Start the Drum
Start the Dance
Start the Show of Masculine Expression
Nurtured in Feminine Creative Seas
Roll like Thunder
Ring Rattle Bell
Ring Rattle Blow Whistle
for Sons Ring Rattle
for Sons' Smiles Ring Rattle
for Sons' Talk Ring Rattle
for Sons' Strength Ring Rattle
for Sons' Thoughts Ring Rattle
for Sons' Blessings Ring Rattle
for Sons
for Sons
for Sons
Ring Rattle

Poet's Eye

For Imani Rose Daughter Girl

Woman eyes aware
Warrior spirit burns in heart
Rhythm never stops
Rhythm never stops
She of the eternal
Sister dance
Shall know her name
And believe
That we are truly free
Only in the spirit of us
Celebratin' us
Rhythm never stops
Rhythm Never Stops
RHYTHM NEVER STOPS!

Imani is the Kiswahili word for Faith, especially celebrated on the final day of Kwanzaa (January 1). "Poet's Eye" was written the day of Imani's birth (8/30/92). Darius (born 2/17/98), Imani's brother, is celebrated in "Clave for Son" written on Father's Day (6/21/98). The clave is the essential element in Afro-Cuban drumming and music. Both of these poems were created on Sundays in Malcolm X Park on 16th Street in Washington, DC where traditionally drummers, dancers, and the cultural community have gathered for decades and where African Liberation Day has been celebrated through the spirit of Kwame Toure aka Stokely Carmichael. May we be forever blessed.

Dezombification of a Mommy

For Mary on Mother's Day 5/13/07

She greets the dawn and daughter
in vitalized upright purposeful movements.
Jerked to life
out of a warm crypt
of silk, quilts and cotton
she rises to bird calls,
Carolina wrens in argument,
towhees cheering
another moment on Earth,
and commotions
in other rooms, teen daughter slowly risen,
damage control and calls
to defeat new day haze.
Water trickles from the sky
make molasses of the mind.
A best blessed meal
must be sent through
to the daughter's soul
or her dance that day
will be offbeat and uncool.
A global dooming ensues
with the bus and knowledge missed,
a kiss of galactic disruption.
The mommy acts,
the universe now safe
with daughter girl delivered
in the tick of chime.
Unbalanced spirit returns home
to regain quiet time,

an Erzuli momma posed
before a red orange blue flame
accepts the directive,
meditates and recharges
for her next missions
- the untoothbrushing son,
firestopping communications,
and that late night desirous husband.
As drums beat
midnight mockingbirds sing,
sweet fermentations are sipped
and a soul rests
possessed at play
again in rose petals.

ST. JOSEPH'S HISTORIC FOUNDATION/HAYTI HERITAGE CENTER
presents
"SCIENCEQUEST," A MUSICAL THAT CELEBRATES SCIENCE IN THE TRIANGLE THROUGH ART
Artistic Director, Tony Small
Science Director, Darrell Stover
Director, Jasme' Kelly
Choreographer, Toya Chinfloo
Set Design, Algenon Conyers
Costume Design, Candace Staten
Musical Accompaniment by the North Carolina Jazz Ensemble
And featuring the children of ArtsQuest Summer Camp 2000
and their Adult Mentors
FRIDAY, JULY 28TH 7:00 PM and
SATURDAY, JULY 29TH 3:00 PM
John Freidrick Educational Technology Complex Auditorium at the
North Carolina School of Science and Mathematics
Corner of Maryland Avenue and West Club Boulevard, Durham, NC.
(DONATIONS WELCOME)
THIS ENLIGHTENING STAGE PERFORMANCE WILL LIFT THE IQ'S
OF ITS AUDIENCE BY AT LEAST 30 POINTS!!!!!!!!!!!!!!!!!!
For more information call 683-1709
www.hayti.org

Thing Hip Hop

For Guru

The debate was settled
Hip Hop ain't what they say
Neither are you
Your beats your verbs
Hip Hop vital
Guttenberg bible
Magna Carta
Declaration of Independence
All heaved to alley heat and roarin' winds friend
Brown baby face blasted
Manifesto of resistance
Griot dozens master
Snappin' fangs
Whippin' tongues
Twistin' feets
Kickin' scientific rap innovations
Spectral sprays of a new nation
Conceived in neglect
A new nation
Misperceived
Caught-up young dummies
Off key adults
Victim commodities
A new nation
Sovereign chocolate urbanness
Hearty high times on hard surfaces
Translated pain
All in the percenter flow, yo
A new nation

Battlin' inside and outside an imposed otherness
Dismissed victimness
Criminalized youthfulness
A new nation
New gods
Under siege
You spit the charge
We raise up a billion boomboxes
Eternally refreshed batteries
Connected in sizzle time
Power quakes and shakes us
As neurons crackle and spark
Providin' thing hip hop new script
Steady flip pumpin' sizzle pulse
Out the gutter of mother goose banter
Corporate induced zombie chatter
Magician jali in the tradition of bomb speak
Sparkin' parties
Sizzlin' street creeds
A new nation
Bridge builder between your days' beboppers
And the hip hoppers of an Ellingtonian Monkish
Basied Dizzy Miles Max beat era
Called them back to the past
Sankofa howl
Skill kid
Got your rep and cred
Old soul
Back from the forward time
Looped in the past
Graduated in street tense givens
Master of the ancestor shout out
It's both how and what is said
Today's know nothings need to check your bins
Delta blues to Chicago riddles and rhymes
Sifted through Harlem alleys

Different shades of true Brooklyn Black
No slack in your attack
Called them back
Hollered
Warned them
America eats its know nothings
Haunted and scared
Wicked and word weak
Holdin' blank white paper
With no heart
Can be saved
Glowin in the light
Saturated phrase by phrase
Sailin' on the arc of your jazz thing
Ancestors called, y'all
They told Guru to tell you
Come back
Come back
Somewhere deep down when
Don't let them thing you to death
Your black body is alive,
Valuable and beautiful to us
Get your butts back here!
Come baaaack!

Too Funky Tooo Funky

For Betty Davis and Chaka Khan

SHE
ALL SPELLED IN CAPS
IS THEIR NAME
IN DAISY DUKE SHORTS
AND MINIATURIZED STRIPS
ONLY BARELY RESEMBLING SKIRTS.
IT ALL SHAKES
RIGHT IN RHYTHM
TO AN UNHEARD BEAT
FEELING GOOD TO THE EYES.
BAM AND THERE IT IS!
AGAIN FOR THE 100TH TIME TODAY!
A NOISE IN THE FOREFRONT
AND SURROUNDING SOME NASTY STUFF
GOING ON IN MY MIND
AFTER SEEING THE DAZZLE OF THIGH, SMILE
AND ALL THAT SPACY SACREDNESS
SPICED WITH UNHTELLECT!
BABY BURN
BEFORE WE ALL COOL OUT.
SCORCH THE SIDE EFFECT OF APATHY
FOR WE MUST DANCE!
TO DO NOTHING
ASIDE FROM QUIETLY SIT
AND BABBLE IS A SIN
AGAINST THE SOUND.
THE GROUND

UNSTOMPED AND PROWLED
BY SOUL-SHAKING FEMININITY
IS SOIL
WITH NO LIFE -- JUST UNSACRED DIRT.

I Need Me a Bic Pen Poem

For Willie Vasquez`

I Need A Bic Pen for my Guiro
I Need A Bic Pen for my Shicka AShicka AShicka Shick!
The Pleasure of the Sound is Essential
To the Spirit of the People
I Need A Bic Pen for my Guiro
I Need A Bic Pen for my Shicka AShicka AShicka Shick!
The Right Soundin' Beat is Where It's At!
Sittin' All in the Pocket You Know!
I Need A Bic Pen for my Guiro
I Need A Bic Pen for my Shicka AShicka AShicka Shick!
Fillin' the Air, the Mind, and the Heart
With a Challenge to Dance!
I Need A Bic Pen for my Guiro
I Need A Bic Pen for my Shicka AShicka AShicka Shick!
Something 'Bout that Hexagonal Shape
Gets Inside You and Rattles and Shakes
Step to the Floor!
No Virgin, You've Been There Before!
Escuche!
I Need A Bic Pen for my Guiro
I Need A Bic Pen for my Shicka AShicka AShicka Shick!
A Pen Not for Writing
A Pen for Playing
Saying - BAILE!
Listen to My Rhythm
TODO EL MUNDO BAILA!
I Need A Bic Pen for my Guiro
I Need A Bic Pen for my Shicka AShicka AShicka Shick!
I Need A Bic Pen for my Guiro

I Need A Bic Pen for my Shicka AShicka AShicka Shick!
Shicka AShicka AShicka Shick!
Shicka AShicka AShicka Shick!

You Are Invited to

A Pre-Kwanzaa Celebration

A Community Cultural Colaboration

Presented by the African American Dance Ensemble and Community Artists

at

The John Avery Boys & Girls Club

808 E. Pettigrew St.

Durham, NC

on

December 11, 1996

at 5 p.m.

In the Spirit of Imani (Faith)

Featuring:

African American Dance Ensemble Artist:
Andrew Daniels II, Fahali Igbo, Gail Rouse, Ashi Smythe Sr.,

Community Artist:
Darrell Stover

And all the youthful energy of the children at the club!

The whole village will be involved in
Music, Dance, Song & Poetry
THIS EVENT IS FREE

How Deep Can You Be?

Deeper than an ocean bottom of bones
Deeper than Mississippi mud
Deeper than the sky is high
Deeper than the Nile is long
    the blues in Jazz
    the total sex performed in millennia passed
Deep
Deeper than negrophobia and Jim Crow
Deeper than Blaxploitation saving Hollywood
    Rap saving the record industry
    and Hip Hop saving Wall Street
Deeper than Spike Lee and Prince on a good day, De La Soul,
    and the Thug Life of Tupac Shakur
Deep
Deeper than Dubois, now that's deep
Deeper than Frederick Douglass, now you talking
Deeper than the NAACP, Rosa Parks and all them tired feet
Deeper than Angela Davis's 'fro
    Pam Grier's beauty in perpetuity
    Assata Shakur's freedom
    Mumia's appeal
Deeper than anything happening to them
Deeper than Iraq, Afghanistan, Pakistan and Haiti
    WTO No! People Yes!
    The Fire This Time!
    Vive Vessey!
Deeper than African banjos
played at American presidential inaugurations
Deep
Deeper than Fannie Lou Hamer, proud, loud and strong
Deeper than Lumumba, Fanon and negritude

Deeper than Juneteenth, post-colonial past puppets
    Reconstruction Apartheid Free Africa
Deeper than Bahia, the bottomless pit of Driving While Black
police brutality and harassment, crack meth Bush ghetto gun
    running Just Say No to more MTV versions of America
    hooked on itself and BET versions of Blacks hooked on
    nothing
Deep
Deeper than deep
Deeper than how low can you go
Deeper than get down, get down
Deeper than Barry White's basso profundo
    Luther Vandross's pleas
    Minnie Ripperton's peaks
    and Little Kim's repentances
Deep
Deeper than Mars missions lost
    to martians that didn't offer the invitation
    Bermuda squares, circles and triangles
Deeper than dinosaurs,
comets and gene therapy for ambidexterity
Deeper than pyramids in Ohio and Olmec heads in China
Deeper than Amiri Baraka, Jane Cortez
    Sonia Sanchez, Niki Giovanni and Luis Rodriguez
Deeper than the funky deep end of the pool at 4 years old
Deeper than the Vatican and Voudou
Deeper than the Himalayas are tall
Deeper than one trillion computers computing one zillion
equations in one googol of a second
Deep
Deeper than Clinton's passion for Lewinsky
Deeper than the street bred pens of Iceberg Slim and Bukowski
Deeper than the mind field of a library on final exam eve
Deeper than hiding on the Underground Railroad
needing to sneeze
Deeper than Harriet Tubman

shooting you if you wanted to go back
Deeper than God's creation by evolution's miscalculations,
    a homeboy's life taken over some fly gear,
    genocide here, there and there
Deeper than speaking all the languages on the planet at one time
    saying DEEP so loud
    the universe flips to brown on the other side
    simmering into a tasty salmon cake
    eaten by the grandmother of God
    washed down her deep throat
    with grape Kool-Aid
    spilled on the obituary
    of the last poet
Deep...

www.ingramcontent.com/pod-product-compliance
Ingram Content Group UK Ltd.
Pitfield, Milton Keynes, MK11 3LW, UK
UKHW041941190726
13854UKWH00004B/1719

9 780557 859122